INTR(

Jesus is about so much more tha die. One of His mission statements is, i nave come that you may have (that I might impart to you) abundant life" (John 10:10b). When He called His first disciples, He promised, "I will make you (grow you into) … " (Matthew 4:18). His desire is to help us grow into the unique, whole, healed, complete person He had in mind when He dreamed us up and then called us to Himself. We all want to experience MORE of Jesus in our every-day-ness. We want a relationship with Jesus that works … that is real and relevant today. That's the hope of these 30 quiet times.

Much of Christian discipleship today views our spirituality as a static possession rather than as a dynamic, ever developing, growth toward wholeness in Jesus. Many view discipleship as my spiritual life, as an "endless quest for techniques, methods, and programs by which we hope to achieve spiritual fulfillment." This premise for spiritual growth puts us in charge of growing our relationship with Jesus as we strive to "get closer to Jesus." Experiencing more of Jesus cannot be done by us — by our effort. It's a journey in our ever-deepening response to God, Whose purpose shapes our heart and life's direction, Whose grace redeems our wayward choices, Whose power liberates us from the wounds and corresponding bondage of our past, Whose Holy Spirit heals our brokenness, Whose forgiveness totally cleanses us, and Whose love for us is the most real thing about us. Experiencing more of Jesus is our deepening trust in His love for us and our increasing responsiveness to His imparting life to us as He grows us into wholeness.

Therefore, experiencing more of Jesus is received as a gift from God. However, we must bring great intention to the relationship, without which our growth will be retarded. A way to think about our intention is to "greenhouse our souls." In a greenhouse, we create the best possible environment to enable a plant to grow. We ensure the best fertilizer and soil, light and temperature, water and pruning. But, it is God who grows the plant (1 Corinthians 3:6-7). When we greenhouse our souls, we create the best environment to experience more of Jesus. The best fertilizer, soil, water, temperature and more are our spiritual disciplines, like those presented in the last 15 days of this book. We make the greenhouse, but it is God who grows us.

This book is organized in three sections: "The Foundation of Spiritual Formation," "Realities of Spiritual Formation," and "Spiritual Disciplines for Spiritual Formation." These Scriptures, God's words, and my accompanying human words, come with the prayer that the Holy Spirit would drop any good words into your hearts and blow any unhelpful words away, like chaff in the wind. Please read God's words before reading my words, because God's words will have much more impact than mine. It takes time to turn in the Bible to locate God's words, but it is absolutely worth your time. The other prayer is that this written effort would truly help you experience more of Jesus daily, even moment by moment.

Ty Saltzgiver
March 2017

TABLE OF CONTENTS

THE FOUNDATION OF SPIRITUAL FORMATION

Day 1   The Gospel of Jesus
Day 2   Jesus is Everything
Day 3   Seized by the Power of God's Great Affection
Day 4   When Jesus Calls a Person, He Bids Them
to Come and Die ... Dietrich Bonhoeffer
Day 5   Choosing Trust
Day 6   God's Always Thinking of You
Day 7   Our Lens Through Which We View Our Relationship With Jesus
Day 8   O Lord, Come to my Assistance. Lord, Make Haste to
Help Me...Psalm 20:1
Day 9   Our Soul and Its Desire

REALITIES OF SPIRITUAL FORMATION

Day 10   Hindrances and Our Enemy
Day 11   Desiring and Nurturing Humility
Day 12   The Grace of Receiving
Day 13   True Self ... False Self ... Our Identity
Day 14   The Place of Suffering
Day 15   Attention to Our Heart

SPIRITUAL DISCIPLINES FOR SPIRITUAL FORMATION

Day 16   "If You Are Truly My Disciples, You Will Abide in
My Word" ... Jesus
Day 17   A Way of Listening to God with Scripture ... *Lectio Divina*
Day 18   A Way of Entering Into God's Word With Jesus
Day 19   A Way of Hiding God's Word in Your Heart
Day 20   Our Journey Into Intimacy With God ... Prayer
Day 21   Centering Prayer
Day 22   A Prayer Walk
Day 23   Developing Spiritual Friends ... Community
Day 24   The Furnace of Transformation ... Solitude and Silence
Day 25   Acknowledging Our Sin Before God ... Confession
Day 26   Granting Forgiveness to Another (or to Oneself)
Day 27   Keeping Our Memory Alive
Day 28   Practicing the Presence of God ... The Daily Examen
Day 29   Giving our Life Away
Day 30   Cultivating Gratitude

EPILOGUE AND BLESSING

The Foundation of Spiritual Formation
THE GOSPEL OF JESUS

Colossians 1:13-14, 22-23 | 2 Corinthians 5:21

When we moved to Colorado Springs in 2001, and I saw we were living at the base of majestic Pikes Peak, I promised myself that I would never take that view for granted. I would always hold it in awe. Basically, I've kept that promise; however, there are days I don't look up and notice its beauty. The activity of the day pushes Pike Peak from front burner to back burner to even off the stove. We can fall into that "not looking up" mode with the Gospel of Jesus. Do we hold the Gospel in awe, noticing its beauty and effect every day? Do we daily marvel that God rescued us for Himself at the greatest of costs – His own Son's death?

God brought into being all created things — the oceans and dry land, all the animals, the sun, moon and stars, etc. It was and is ALL good, ALL with His imprint. Then He made us humans, not just with His imprint, but in His VERY IMAGE (Genesis 1:27, 31). We weren't just good, but God said we were and are VERY GOOD (***tauv maude*** — Hebrew idiom in Genesis 1:31 meaning God was giddy, beside Himself with joy and excitement). Here was the created being He would enjoy relating to, even visiting daily with them "in the cool of the afternoon" (Genesis 3:8). We are made to enjoy God, and for Him to be our Source of life.

Adam and Eve's story is our story, their experience is our experience. The Garden of Eden represents God giving us all His goodness, and showing His deep desire and joy in being with us. But, we want to be the god of our life; we have difficulty trusting God for everything; we think there must be more to life than God is allowing us to experience; so, we choose to break trust with God and go our own way (Genesis 3:7-10; 6:5-6). In our hearts, we turn away from God to take control of our lives. The Bible calls this "sin."

The consequence of our sin nature is not the freedom we crave; rather we are subject to darkness, controlled by what we attach to in hopes of more life, and enslaved by our fears. In short, we experience death — literal death and spiritual death. Our relationship with God is poisoned. We are alienated from God (Colossians 1:21). Part of the hell of it is that we can do absolutely nothing to fix, heal, or overcome our sin and its consequences. But, what we couldn't do ourselves, God did for us. He sent His Son, Jesus. We are Jesus' most treasured possession, and in His love and His longing to be in right relationship with us, He gave His life on the cross to remove our sin from us, clearing the way for us to be in that right relationship with Him.

Every verse in the Bible that speaks of our sin and us experiencing its devastating effects, also speaks of God's rescue. It's as if when God was writing the Scripture, He couldn't wait to share His solution every time the reality of sin was shared. Each verse has a **glorious comma**:

Isaiah 53:6 ... "We all like sheep have gone astray, each of us has turned to his own way, and the Lord has laid on Him the iniquity of us all."

3

Romans 3:23-24 … "For all have sinned and fall short of the glory of God, and are justified freely by His grace through the redemption that came by Jesus."

Romans 6:23 … "For the wages of sin is death, but the free gift of God is eternal life in Christ Jesus our Lord."

Ephesians 2:5 … "When we were dead in our transgressions, God made us alive with Christ."

Colossians 1:21-22 … "Once we were alienated from God and His very enemies because of our evil behavior, but now He has reconciled us to God by Christ's physical body through death, in order to present us before God, holy, without blemish, and free from accusation."

In Jesus' death on the cross, He didn't just forgive our sin or grant us a pardon from its full consequence; He actually bore our sin. He **became** sin. In the GREAT EXCHANGE, Jesus' righteousness was imparted to us, and our sin, along with all the guilt, shame and self-condemnation (Romans 8:1-4) that accompanies it, is transferred to Jesus. It was as if the Father had a giant sponge and simultaneously absorbed out of every one of us across time ALL of our sin and wrung it out on Jesus on the cross. Jesus is our substitute, experiencing what we deserved in relationship with God — alienation and death (Isaiah 53:5).

ALL was accomplished by Jesus to make our relationship with God right again. In John 19:28-30, when Jesus said, "It is finished," it was in the present perfect future tense. It should be translated that Jesus' sacrifice on our behalf, "has been and will forever remain finished." We simply need to receive this gift from God. God initiates with us. "Even the desire to turn to God … this too is a gift from God" (St. Augustine). God has the scales fall from our eyes to see Jesus, and the crust breaks around our hearts to receive Jesus (Ephesians 2:8-9; Titus 3:4-5). We respond to His invitation of total forgiveness and union with Him, by giving all that we know of ourselves, to all that we know of Him, and by asking Him to come live in our hearts (Colossians 1:27; Ephesians 3:17).

This wonderful reality, Jesus, who is resurrected and alive today, who upholds the universe by the power of His Word, who created ALL things, who knit us together in our mother's womb, actually lives in our hearts and is the beginning of our spiritual formation. Never lose our awe of Him. Never cease looking up and marveling at the Gospel of Jesus … **FOR YOU AND ME.**

Other Scripture:
Mark 1:15; John 3:16; Acts 2:36; Romans 1:16-17; Romans 10:9-12; 1 John 1:5

Jesus is Everything
Philippians 3:7-11 | Luke 4:17-21 (Isaiah 61:1-4)

If our relationship with Jesus has grown staid or dry, lacking vitality and depth, not going anywhere, even become a bit boring as we go through the

4

religious motions, then we've lost our focus on Jesus Christ. As Thomas Merton said, "When we start seeking something else besides Jesus, we lose it. This is His call to us — simply to be people who are content to live close to Jesus and renew the kind of life in which the closeness is felt and experienced." The Apostle Paul rightly says that knowing Jesus is the surpassing greatness of his life. He goes on to say that every wonderful thing he has experienced in life is as "horse manure" when compared to knowing Jesus. Is that unique to Paul? Or, could that be reality for us as well?

Jesus calls us not to a belief system or a moral code, but to **HIMSELF**. **"FOLLOW ME"** is Jesus' most used invitation to discipleship (used 69 times in the Bible). The usual Greek word translated **follow** is **akoloutho**, which means much more than to imitate or copy. It means to attach to, to apprentice with, to live with and learn about life with Jesus; to connect with Him like a branch does to the vine (John 15:4-5). When we accept Jesus' invitation to attach to and apprentice with Him, He makes us a promise, like He did when He called Peter (Matthew 4:18-20). He says, "I will make you … ." We have a sense that God made each one of us … that we are "fearfully and wonderfully made" (Psalm 139:13-14). Yet, do we have an equal sense that God is still making us? It's the truth communicated in Philippians 1:6. "You can be confident of this: He who began a good work in you, will see it through to completion." He will grow us into the unique, whole, image-bearer He dreamed up, before He even knit us together in our mother's womb (Jeremiah 2:5).

Jesus is the "author and perfector" of our spiritual formation (Hebrews 12:2). He said in John 10:10 that His **raison d'etre** is to impart to us **abundant life**. There are numerous Greek words for life; for instance, **bios** is physical life, and **psyche** refers to emotional life. This word for **life** in John 10:10 is **zoe**, which means the life that comes from God, the Inventor and Source of all Life. The adjective we translate as **ABUNDANT** is **perosis**. It means that you pour water to fill up a cup. When the cup is full, you keep on pouring, so that it continuously overflows. It is continuously more than needed. It's life to the full, and then more. Jesus uses another adjective to describe **zoe** in John 17:3 — **aionis**. We translate **aionis** as "eternal," which can tend to miss its meaning. Eternal is so much more than a time reference of "from now to forever." **Aionis** is a deep quality of life, or a rich character of life. It is best translated as a deep, rich, lasting life. Jesus goes on in John17:3 to give the definition of **aionis zoe** as simply this: "that you **KNOW** the one True God, and Jesus Christ whom He has sent." The Greek word we translate as **KNOW** is **ginoskein**, which means not just to have knowledge about someone; rather, it is the most intimate way of knowing another. It is becoming intertwined with or knit together. "Adam **KNEW** Eve and they conceived a son" is the same root word. I Peter 1:17 declares rightly that we share a "divine nature" with Jesus. Jesus prayed about this union with Himself in John 17:21, "Help them (us) be one, just as You are in Me, and I in You, may they be in Us." This intimate, intertwined, **ginoskein** of Jesus, to whom we apprentice to, is the basis of our spiritual formation to experience the **zoe** we so desire.

Jesus announced His ministry in the synagogue in Nazareth describing the **perosis zoe** and **aionis zoe** He so desires us to have (Luke 4:17-20). He wants us to see clearly with His eyes, not our culturally programmed eyes, to be free from whatever holds us captive, to be released from whatever burdens us (worries, fears, bitterness, unforgiveness, etc.), and to be healed of our wounded hearts. It is Jesus' greatest pleasure to impart His **zoe** to us, delivering on His promise: "I will make you … " from the unique position of His residence in our hearts.

This is what Hudson Taylor, the great missionary to the Far East, meant when he said that his "spiritual secret" was "drawing for every need, whether temporal or spiritual, upon 'the fathomless wealth of Jesus'" (Ephesians 3:8).This is why the Apostle Paul said everything in his life is as horse manure when compared to knowing (**ginoskein**) Jesus. Do we really believe Jesus is enough for the life we crave and pursue? Our spiritual formation is our journey into union with Jesus … our self deeply centered in, attached to, and abandoned to Jesus.

Other Scripture:
Matthew 6:33; Luke 15:31; John 4:13-14; John 5:39-40, MSG; John 7:37-38; John 15:5; Acts 17:28; Romans 8:32

 DAY 3

Seized by the Power of God's Great Affection

Exodus 34:6 | Isaiah 43:1-5 | Ephesians 3:14-19

Can we try the old psychiatrist's office game? What's the first word that pops into your head (without thinking) when we hear the word, "GOD"? Would we say "Creator," or "Infinite," or "Omniscient (omni-everything)," or … ? How many of us would blurt out, "My Lover," not just Love, but the One who loves me like no other.

"What comes into our minds when we think about God is THE MOST IMPORTANT thing about us … the most portentous fact about any person is not what he (or she) may say or do, but what she (or he) at any given moment in his (her) deep heart conceives God to be like." — A.W. Tozer

God wants to be known as our Lover. From the beginning of His revealing Himself, God spoke primarily of His compassionate and loving heart toward us. To His chosen people, the Hebrew nation, God gave a credo to repeat about who He (Yahweh) is. They taught their children using this credo. It is the Exodus reference above. David, named "a man after God's own heart," wrote of God's love 175 times in the Psalms — by far the most prominent theme of his writing. Consider Psalm 63:3 … "Your love for me is better than life itself." The prophets (Isaiah above; Jeremiah 31:3; Hosea 2:19; Zephaniah 3:16-17 and many more), Song of Solomon (7:10), the Apostle Paul (Ephesians above and Romans 8:38-39), John (1 John 4:19) and Jesus Himself (John 15:13), all shared and lived the same reality of God: He loves me without any conditions, boundaries, limits, or breaking point. God's love for us is, as Paul says, "a love beyond any human understanding" (Ephesians 3:19). What ultimately convinces us that God unashamedly loves us is Jesus screaming to us from the cross, "I'm here out of My love for you" (Romans 5:8; Hebrews 12:2).

If our primary conception of God does not hold a prominent place for Him as our Lover, then our view of Almighty God will default dangerously close to the Christmas jingle: "He sees you when you're sleeping; He knows when you're awake; He knows if you've been bad or good; so, be good for goodness sake." And, spiritual formation gravitates to earning God's favor and to shaping our lives to be more righteous and spiritual.

Why is knowing God as our Lover essential in our spiritual formation? Martin Luther reflects on this: "If a person is converted because of fear (of any kind: hell, death, punishment, God is harsh, fickle, etc.), that person will eventually hate their conversion; but if converted because of love, they will love their conversion, and want to grow into it." The Apostle Paul adds that when we know (**ginoskein** — Day 2) God's love, we are "filled with the fullness of God" (Ephesians 3:19). Perhaps Jesus' greatest definition of discipleship is: "As the Father loves Me, that's how I love you … now, abide in My love" (John 15:9). Receiving God's love and making our home in it, and letting His extravagant love penetrate our hearts, is the operative principle in our spiritual formation. Spiritual formation does not happen by practicing spiritual disciplines — that's the Pharisees, the older brother in Luke 15's Prodigal Son parable, and maybe Martha in Luke 10; rather, spiritual formation happens by letting ourselves be loved by God.

Brennan Manning tells the story of his walking with a monk early one morning while on a weeklong retreat. Brennan was pouring out his heart to the monk, when the monk stopped and was staring straight ahead, daydreaming, eyes glazed over. Brennan moved his hand in front of the monk's face saying, "Where were you, Padre?" A smile came over the monk's face as he said, "Ah, the Heavenly Father is awfully fond of me this morning." Julian of Norwich once wrote: "The greatest honor we can give God is to live gladly, knowing we are loved by Him."

The title of today, "Seized by the Power of a Great Affection" was the phrase used in the early 1800s by the slave community around New Orleans, as their phrase describing someone who had given their life to Jesus. For instance, today we might say, "I was saved," or, "I began my relationship with Jesus," or, "I came to faith." They referred to conversion as "being seized by the power of God's great affection."

Other Scripture:
Psalm 36:8; Psalm 52:8; Psalm 59:17; Psalm 86:5,13; Lamentations 3:22-23; Mark 14:3-6, 9

  ## "When God Bids a Person Come, He Bids Them to Come and Die." — Dietrich Bonhoeffer

Matthew 13:44 | Psalm 51:17 | Galatians 2:20

In the popular poker game Texas Hold 'Em, there comes a time when you have to decide, "Am I going to go 'all-in'?" You bet all your chips, all you have;

you risk everything, because you believe you have the best hand to win. It must be that way with our souls. We must go "all-in" with our lives with Jesus for our spiritual formation to continue.

Jesus was clear about this.

"A relationship with Me is like a treasure hidden in a field, which a man found and hid; and from joy over it he goes and sells **all that he has**, in order to possess that field and its treasure" (Matthew 13:44).

"If anyone wishes to come after Me, let them deny themselves and **take up their cross, daily**, and follow Me" (Luke 9:23; Matthew 10:38).

" … unless a grain of wheat falls into the earth and **dies**, it remains by itself alone, but if it **dies**, it bears much fruit" (John 12:24).

Also Matthew 8:19-22; Luke 9:24, 57-62; Mark 8:35; John 15:5

Paul was also clear in Galatians 2:20 above; in Philippians 3:7-8; in Romans 6:3-11, 12:1.

We believe in Jesus and want **MORE** of Him. We are so grateful He came to Earth to reveal the compassionate heart of The Father and to die bearing our sin, thus removing it from us, so that we can have an actual relationship with God of union. But, we stop there. We hold back on the "**all-in**," **everything, our whole self,** part. Are we not certain Jesus is life and will impart to us life-to-the-full (**perosis** and **aionis zoe** – Day 2)? Are we hedging our bet? C.S. Lewis said, "If Jesus' claims are false, then they are of no importance, and if they are true, they are of infinite importance. The one they cannot be is only moderately important."

We readily admit God saved us (we couldn't on our own), but then we effectively say, "I'll take it from here. Doesn't God help those who help themselves?" We are like Peter on Jesus' last night (recorded in Matthew 26:31-35), who literally ignores Jesus' words and declares what he will do, given his own interpretation of the situation and relying on his own strength. Is it too demanding to ask us to put self aside, and move Jesus to the center? Is it an unfair, basically impossible request from Jesus to die to self (that's what "pick up your cross" means), to die to our personal desires and ambitions, so that we can live into Jesus? Won't we lose our essence, our personality, our life? But consider this: Does the Potter (God) dehumanize the clay (us)? No. Our choice, our will, our destiny, our personality is not taken away; it's quite the opposite. Jesus' love and His Spirit within us bestows worth and glory on us. He enables our true self to emerge. He leads us in writing our life story, which far exceeds what we could have written on our own (Isaiah 64:1).

It is our most difficult spiritual task to die to self, to give up control, and to surrender our whole self to Jesus. Isaac Watts wrote the hymn "When I Survey the Wondrous Cross," which contains the lyric, "Love so amazing, so divine, demands my soul, my life, my all." That is why G.K. Chesterton said, "Jesus has not been tried and left wanting, rather surrendering to Jesus is difficult and left untried." Going "**all-in**" with Jesus is a prerequisite of our spiritual formation. As we move from childhood through adolescence to adulthood, it is a movement from dependence to independence. With our spiritual formation, it's exactly the opposite. We move from independence from, to dependence on, Jesus.

Choosing Trust

Proverbs 3:5-6 | John 6:28-29 | John 14:1

What was going through Eve's mind and heart as she chose to break trust with God on that ill-fated day in the Garden of Eden (because, are we any different?)? Was it that she wanted to be like God (the beginning of our bent to self-sufficiency) ... Genesis 3:4-6? Did she doubt God's Word as Satan contradicted God saying, "You shall not surely die ... in fact, you'll be like a god" (the beginning of our believing Satan's lies about God [or about us] as if they were truth)? Was she thinking, "This garden and the life and purpose God has given us is surely wonderful; but, there must be more life out there we need to experience" (the beginning of our being wooed to go after the things of this world [Mark 4:18-19, 1 John 2:15-16] for the **MORE** of life, instead of the **MORE** of Jesus being all we could ever need or imagine in life)? All these oppose our choice to trust God. Plus, we can add to them that most of us have experienced a betrayal of trust, and then we have a wounded heart, which we must protect at all costs. Some of us have experienced suffering (see Day 14) in a way that our pain supersedes any sense of God's presence with us, leading us to think: How can I trust a God if He allows that pain? Trusting God isn't an easy, natural choice.

We cannot trust anyone unless we know their heart. Is their heart pure and true, with love and absolute good intention toward me? We can see Jesus' heart is worthy of our trust in the Gospels, and our experience of His heart for us builds our ability to daily choose to trust Him. When someone dies for you, you no longer question their intentions toward you. The Apostle Paul captures this: "He who did not spare His own Son, but delivered Him up for us all, how much more will He not graciously give us ALL THINGS along with Him" (Romans 8:32). As you let God love you, and your heart is "seized by the power of His great affection"(Day 3), trust happens. Trusting our heart into God's care is our response to being loved.

Jesus knew that trusting Him is central to a deepening relationship with Him and to our spiritual formation. When He was asked straight up, "What shall we do, that we might be sure to do the work that God wants?" Jesus' answer was unmistakably clear, "This is the work of God (better translated, the work God does), that you trust Him who He has sent" (John 6:28-29). The Greek word translated **trust** in English is *pisteuo*. It often appears in the Bible as "believe," but that diminishes its meaning. *Pisteuo* doesn't just mean intellectual assent to something; it also carries with it the corresponding action. For instance, to say, "I *pisteuo* that the pond's ice is thick enough to hold me," is actually to be out walking on the pond. *Pisteuo* is more like trusting than believing. Jesus is essentially saying, "The main work that pleases God and benefits you the most, is trusting Me." Trust binds my heart to Jesus' heart.

None of us goes through life "trustless," meaning we all trust in someone (usually ourselves), or in something, in the hope of our fulfillment, happiness, and life-to-the-full. Our choosing to trust Jesus is not once-for-all-time, as we never arrive at trusting. It's a daily, hourly, even moment by moment choosing. The trouble with us "living sacrifices" (Romans 12:1) is that we keep getting down off the altar. The life without trusting in Jesus gravitates to worry, anxiety and fear. Trusting Jesus is never doubt free, just like having courage is never fear free. We can pray as the disciples cried out, "Lord, increase our trust" (Luke 17:5).

Sometimes our choosing to trust God is in the crucible of life, like it was for Job (Job 13:14-15). At the height of his pain, loss, confusion, apparent abandonment by God and persecution at the hands of his so-called friends, he chose trust, "Should I take my life into my own hands? Even though He slays me, I will trust in him." When Jesus' soul was so "troubled to the point of death," sweating drops of blood instead of perspiration, He chose trust, "Not my will, but yours, Father" (Matthew 26:42). A short while later, when Jesus was in extreme physical pain and bearing the worst — the sense of the Father's abandonment — He again chose trust, "Into Your hands I entrust My spirit" (Luke 23:46). Sometimes our choosing to trust God is in the full knowledge of God's love and power for our sake, "As for me, I choose to trust the One who willed to save me, knew the way to do it, had the power to carry it out, and did so for my salvation" (Bernard of Clairvaux). "To not trust that God is powerful and can do works on our behalf, which are often incomprehensible to our understanding, is most damaging to the soul" (St. Teresa of Avila). Our choosing to trust God is paramount in our spiritual formation.

Other Scripture: *Genesis 50:20; 2 Kings 18:5; 2 Chronicles 20:20; Psalm 5:11; Psalm 9:9-10; Psalm 13:5-6; Psalm 28:7; Psalm 31:3, 5, 14; Psalm 34:8, 22; Psalm 36:7; Psalm 37:3-5, 7; Psalm 40:4-5; Psalm 56:3-4; Psalm 62:8; Psalm 73:28; Psalm 78:19-22; Psalm 84:11-12; Psalm 112:7; Psalm 116:7; Psalm 118:8-9 Isaiah 8:17; Isaiah 30:15; Matthew 15:28; Luke 7:9, 50; Romans 4:18-25; Hebrews 10:35; Hebrews 11:1-3, 6*

God's Always Thinking of You

Psalm 40:4-5 | Psalm 139:17-18

God thinks about us … not just when we come to mind or when we do something noteworthy for Him, but all the time; not just with an occasional passing thought, but constantly. As the 15th century theologian Angelus Silesius writes, "If God stopped thinking of me, He would cease to exist." So, what does God think about you? If Jesus is sitting across from you in your den, and you know He has full knowledge of everything in your life story — all you are, and all you're not; all your secrets and hidden thoughts and motives are known* to

*To be sure, God knows everything about us. Consider Psalm 94:11; Matthew 9:4; Matthew 10:29-31; and Galatians 4:9. God knowing everything is either the most frightening reality of our lives because we know that we do not measure up to God's standard, and we fear we'll be exposed, held accountable and judged; or, this is the most freeing reality of our lives because it means we don't have to hide or disguise ourselves
10 before God, who knows us better than we even know ourselves and accepts us as we are.

Him; all the times you were a jerk toward someone, or really hurt someone — what do you hear Him say to you? Living into how God truly thinks of us greatly influences our spiritual formation. Let us consider Jesus' heart toward us.

When a woman caught in the very act of adultery is presented to Jesus, He comes to her defense, dismantles the crowd's judgement, and says to her, "Where are your accusers? Does no one condemn you? **NEITHER DO I**" (John 8:10-11). When we are at a low point, it is said about Jesus that "a battered reed He will not break off, and a smoldering wick He will not put out" (Matthew 12:20). Also, consider Psalm 27:13-14 and Psalm 40:1-3. One day, it was as if Jesus said, "Let me tell you a story that shows My Father's heart." And He told the parable we call "The Prodigal Son," but it should be named, "The Extravagant Father" (Luke 15:11-32). In the parable, two wayward sons disappoint and deeply hurt their father, but the father returns unconditional acceptance for their rejection, love for their disdain, and grace instead of calling them into account. That's the heart of God toward us.

The ultimate statement of how Jesus thinks of us is when is He is on the cross. Why is He there? What is His motive to go to the cross? Was He modeling for us utter obedience to the Father's will? Was He just living out His destiny? No. Jesus is on the cross thinking of you and me. It was for "the joy set before Him that He endured the cross and suffered its shame" (Hebrews 12:2). The joy set before Him is being united with you and me in restored relationship.

Most of us sense that God is disappointed with us (because we've messed up), or at least frustrated with us (because we know better). We project on God what we think of ourselves, and we know that we are not worthy of His love or favor. Maybe God was **tauv maude** (Day 1, 2nd paragraph) when He created us, but now I'm hardly "the apple of His eye" (Psalm 17:8), nor am I "daily His delight" (Proverbs 8:35). If we think that God has soured on us, then we believe Satan's lie.

If Jesus is sitting across from you, He would say something like: "Please know that I am always for you, that I believe in you. It brings me joy that you'd let me love you. I am so proud of you. Even though I chose you, you freely choose me. And, with your warts and mess-ups, you haven't thrown in the towel. Even when your belief in me wanes and doubts creep in, you still long for me. I will always patiently restore you when you are down, and I will continue to impart my life to you. Take my yoke upon you and learn from me, for I am gentle and humble of heart."

 # DAY 7 — The Lens Through Which We View Our Relationship With Jesus
Galatians 4:5-7 | John 15:13-17

How do you primarily characterize your relationship with Jesus? We all have some image of how we relate to God, even if unconsciously. The Bible gives us many possibilities:

- We are sheep cared for and led by Jesus, the Good Shepherd (Psalm 23; John 10:11-18).

- We confess to Jesus like Thomas (John 20:28), "My Lord and my God," as His faithful servants (Romans 10:9; Philippians 2:11; I Peter 3:15).

- Jesus is our Creator (Colossians 1:16) and we are created in His image (Genesis 1:27).

- Jesus is the Bridegroom and we are His bride (Luke 5:34-35).

- Jesus is our King and Judge (Matthew 25:34-46), who holds our eternal destiny in His hands, and we are His subjects living to honor our King.

- Jesus is our Lover and we are His beloved (Song of Solomon 7:10; John 13:23).

The view we hold impacts our spiritual formation. May I suggest two others, which we can choose to live into?

1. Jesus caused quite a controversy when He continually called Yahweh, the God of the Universe, His Father — specifically, His Abba. Abba is the Aramaic (Jesus' native language) for "daddy." When Jesus taught us to pray (Luke 11:2), He invited us to address Almighty God with the same, "Abba/daddy." In spite of whatever our experience has been with our flawed earthly fathers and the corresponding baggage that comes with calling God "our Abba," Jesus didn't shy away from revealing God as our Good Father. For many of us, that's the father we've never had. Read Matthew 7:9-11. The apostle John rightfully captured our relating to God as His child in John 1:12: "Yet to all who received Him (Jesus), He gave the right to become a child of God." The Apostle Paul calls us "adopted sons and daughters of God," which also makes us heirs of all the benefits of being family with Jesus (Romans 8:15; 1 John 3:2). When we are family with Jesus, for example, we don't project on God how we experience being an employee with our employer or boss, where if we perform well, we get a raise and a promotion. Nor will our Abba be like a bloodhound sniffing around to discover our sins. Rather, we experience God as our Father, not holding anything back, but freely and excitedly granting us "every spiritual blessing through Jesus" (Ephesians 1:3).

2. It should take our breath away that the same Jesus who's on the throne where the 24 elders never cease saying, "Our Lord and God, you are worthy to receive glory and honor and power, because you have created all things, and by your will they exist and were created." (Revelation 4:10-11), wants to be our friend — **OUR FRIEND**. Read Exodus 33:11. The University of Michigan's Sociology department asked students what their definition of a "best friend" was. The top three answers were: 1. Someone who knows you, the good, the bad, and the ugly, and still accepts you and loves you; 2. Someone who walks with you in the good weather and bad weather of life; and 3. Someone with whom you don't have to measure words. There couldn't be a more accurate portrayal capturing how Jesus is our friend. The desert fathers and mothers called

Jesus their companion in life. **Com** means "with," and **panos** means "bread;" thus, Jesus is the One I break bread with, meaning He's my dearest friend. They spoke of life as "companioning" with Jesus. What a wonderful way to view the "with Jesus" life; that is, our life lived in the reality of Jesus' last words spoken (Matthew 28:20) on earth, "I am with you every moment you live. I am with you when you've had a quiet time and when you haven't, when you feel me near and when you don't, when you've lived well and when you haven't. Every moment means just that — EVERY MOMENT." As we live into being His son or daughter and friend (Philippians 2:13), "Jesus is at work in us, to will and to work according to His good pleasure" (spiritually forming us, so to speak).

DAY 8 — "O Lord, Come to My Assistance, Lord Make Haste to Help Me" — Psalm 70:1

Ezekiel 36:25-27 | 1 Corinthians 3:16 | John 14:16-17, 26

"A person's greatest achievement is to let God help him/her."
— Soren Kirkegaard

It was incomprehensible for the disciples (and for us today) to hear Jesus say, "You ought to be glad I'm going away. It's really to your advantage. For if I do not go away, the Helper (the Paracletos, the One called alongside to help) shall not come to you; but if I go, I will send Him to you" (John 16:7). What could be better than to have Jesus with us every day, leading and teaching us in person about life, about God, and showing us life in action? Jesus says that having the Holy Spirit living in your heart is better. Speaking to a crowd about their "spiritual thirst," He said, "The person who trusts Me will have living water (the Holy Spirit) flowing from their inmost heart" (John 7:37-38).

John the Baptist first described Jesus saying this: "He gives the Spirit without measure" (John 3:34). And, Jesus' first resurrected act was to breathe on His confused and frightened disciples, imparting His Spirit and His Shalom upon them (John 20:19-22). Jesus knows us and "what stuff" we are made of. He knows that even though our spirit is willing (in desiring more of Jesus), our flesh is weak (Mark 14:38). Jesus knows that we need help to draw near to Him, to live true to responding to His love and His invitation into His life. We must abandon our futile efforts to spiritually form ourselves by our sheer will into the Image of Christ. When it comes to experiencing more of Jesus, can we learn to turn to the Spirit now/immediately/always, instead of waiting until after we've exhausted all our own resources?

The Scriptures describe many ways the Spirit helps us, all of which we greatly desire. He brings healing to our hearts, freedom from what holds us captive, release from what oppresses us, and seeing as He does with His eyes (Luke 4:18ff; Isaiah 61:1). The Spirit grows fruit in us of love, joy, peace, patience, kindness, goodness, being faithful, gentleness, and having self-discipline

(Galatians 5:22-23). The Spirit bestows His gift(s) upon each one of us (read 1 Peter 4:10; Romans 12:6-8; 1 Corinthians 12:1-11; Ephesians 4:11-12). We experience conviction of our sin (John 16:8-9) by the Spirit in us. When we don't know how to pray, the Spirit helps us (Romans 8:26-27). We are actually "being changed" into whole, authentic images of Jesus, by the Spirit (2 Corinthians 3:18). The Spirit helps us to worship (John 4:24), and to witness to others of the reality of Jesus (John 15:26-27; Acts 1:8). There's much more, but we can see that the Spirit is absolutely vital to experiencing more of Jesus.

Living life with Jesus and yielding to His Spirit, or "walking by the Spirit" (Galatians 5:16), is a learned art. In fact, it is a continual learning over our lifetime. When we ask Jesus to live in our hearts, we get the Holy Spirit. As we go forward, we don't get more of the Holy Spirit, but we become more aware of the Spirit's active presence.

As we seek, pray for, and join with the Holy Spirit, consider the following two images:

1. A dear friend helped Ann and me put together our wonderful two-week trip to Italy. Ann and I noticed that we had a guide nearly every day. We wondered if we really needed that much input. Would a guide smother our spontaneity, direct us too much and cramp our style? We found it was just the opposite. The guide knew so much about each place, opening us to history and current realities, even sharing with us about multiple restaurants so that we could choose wisely. Jesus actually says that the Spirit will be our guide …"He will guide you into all truth" (John 16:13). He will teach us all things and bring to remembrance all that Jesus has spoken (John 14:26). As a guide, the Spirit will lead us in our path of life (Romans 8:14-16; Psalm 143:10). We learn to listen to Him.

2. Ephesians 5:18 exhorts us "to not get drunk on wine, for that is dissipation; rather, be filled continuously with the Spirit." When we have too much to drink, we are "under the influence" of the alcohol. We are not "in control," but are controlled by the alcohol. It is the same with the Spirit. When we yield to the Spirit, He influences us in everything — in speaking to others, in reading the Scripture, in reasoning and discernment, in living selflessly and more. When we are inebriated with the Spirit, life flows freely and easily.

Other Scripture: *Genesis 1:2; Joel 2:28; Luke 11:13; Romans 5:5; Romans 8:11 1 Corinthians 2:9-14; Ephesians 1:13-14; Ephesians 4:30; 1 Thessalonians 5:19; 1 John 4:13*

Our Soul and Its Desire
Psalm 42:1-2, 4-5 | Matthew 10:28 | Matthew 16:26

All of us readily acknowledge that being made in God's Image means we are, we have, a soul. However, can we articulate what "our soul" is, and why God made us a soul, and what the soul's function is? Our culture throws the word "soul" around with a myriad of meanings, which confuses our understanding of this vital essence of our being. Think of soul music and soul food, soulmates, the expression "bless my soul," and even the distress signal SOS is Save our Souls.

Dallas Willard says, "You are an unceasing spiritual being with an eternal destiny in God's great universe. That's the most important thing about you." Dallas is defining us as primarily a "spiritual being"; in other words, we are souls. Souls are not just a part of us, or something we have; rather, they are us — our essence and the deepest most real part of us. Our soul is given a physical body, and our soul exists after our body dies. It's our soul that cries out to God and our soul where God is most present to us. We experience our deepest pain in our soul. St. John of the Cross speaks of the "dark night of our soul," not of the mind, or of the heart, or of our life. The greatest commandment calls us to love God, with our deepest self, with all our soul (Deuteronomy 6:5; Luke 10:27).

Not surprisingly, as we are made in God's very Image, there are 20 references in the Bible to God's soul. God says to His people, "I will make My dwelling among you, and My soul will not reject you" (Leviticus 26:11). He says to Jesus, "This is My Son, Whom I love; with Him, My soul is well pleased" (Matthew 3:17).

Jesus, whom Peter called "The Shepherd and Guardian of our souls" (1 Peter 2:25), had some profound teaching concerning our souls. He said to yoke with Him in life (it's the easy way), and we will find rest for our souls (Matthew 11:29-30; Psalm 23:3). He warned us to be afraid of him who is able to destroy the soul (Matthew 10:28). But most profound might be His warning that we could gain the whole world and still lose our soul (Matthew 16:25-26). He spoke this warning to His disciples, which means it's not about losing or missing out on salvation; rather, Jesus is saying that nothing is worth more to us than our soul. The soul, by nature, doesn't demand attention. Jesus is warning that in our hurriedness, in our pursuit of other things, and in the demands of life, even of ministry, we can lose touch with our soul. Thus, we lose our connection with God and we lose our healthy center. Our living slides into unreal; our living springs from our ego, or our intellect, or our performing well, rather than from our soul in union with God. This warning from Jesus (and its consequences) should frighten us, and awaken us to care for what we value most highly — our soul.

The soul's greatest function is longing (Psalm 84:2). The soul doesn't long for more knowledge, excitement, pleasure or power. It longs for deep connection with God. Julian of Norwich prayed for the constant wound of continuous longing for Jesus. Our soul was made by God, for God, to need God; so its deepest desire (longing) is to be intimate with God.* This longing is the fuel for any spiritual discipline; otherwise, the disciplines to "greenhouse our soul" presented in this book (Days 16-30) become duty, or a self-help project, or trying to look spiritual. However, if we are truly seeking, "How can I arrange my life for what my soul wants most?," then the disciplines to create a greenhouse become life-giving.

Other Scripture: *Hebrews 6:19; Psalm 16:10; Psalm 19:7; Psalm 25:1, 20; Psalm 31:7; Psalm 33:20; Psalm 41:4; Psalm 49:15; Psalm 54:4; Psalm 57:1; Psalm 62:1; Psalm 63:1, 8; Psalm 66:13; Psalm 103:1-2, 22; Psalm 143:6*

*We have learned to squelch desire in our life, as it has led to harmful things, as James 1:14 describes.

Realities of Spiritual Formation

Receiving the gift from God of experiencing more of Jesus as we die to self and live into Jesus and His life and His way with His Spirit, TAKES TIME. We cannot microwave intimacy with Jesus. And, His timing is unique with each person. Spiritual growth is not a "one size fits all." As we endeavor to experience more of Jesus, it's not a three-step program we complete, nor is it behavior modification (a cosmetic spirituality). Jesus didn't die in our place, making the way for us to have a right relationship with God, so that we'd be nicer people with better morals. Jesus died so that in our right relationship with Him, He could impart **perosis** and **aionis zoe** (Day 2) to us; so that He could "make us" into whole people; and so that the world will know of His real love for them, through us.

Two other realities:

1. We shouldn't try to measure our experiencing more of Jesus. Sometimes, we can see growth in hindsight or when others point it out. Don't become discouraged at a perceived lack of progress. The best action is to savor and enjoy the moments we taste of the Lord's nearness and goodness to us.

2. We cannot expect spiritual disciplines to necessarily overcome and heal trauma that's occurred in our lives (such as a childhood wound). Please allow a counselor to help you work through those emotional or deep psychological issues.

 DAY 10

Hindrances and Our Enemy
1 Peter 5:8-9 | 2 Corinthians 11:3

Nothing in our culture encourages us toward experiencing more of Jesus, toward dying to self and living into Jesus. It's quite the opposite. Our culture seduces us to think power, position, pleasure, popularity, prosperity (wealth), etc., are more essential to life-to-the-full, than more of Jesus is (or, at least, it's Jesus plus those things). Malcolm Muggeridge (the great British statesman) said, "The greatest tragedy which can befall a person is that they would think they are at home in this world." Jesus spoke to how third seed attachments (in Mark 4:18-19) rise up and take hold of our lives. The Apostle John spoke about this reality, too, in 1 John 2:15-16. We are all vulnerable to "drifting" (Hebrews 2:1) away from Jesus, often slowly and undiscernibly.

Add our frantic pace to the allures of this world.* We're compelled by all of our duties of family and job, maintaining a house, practicing hobbies, and pursuing a few friendships. The distractions of media, the noise of constant TV, being tethered to our mobile phones, and keeping up with our sports teams all work against us dedicating time so that we can experience more of Jesus.

Dallas Willard says the key to spiritual growth is to relentlessly eliminate hurry from your life.

Then, there's our DNA of being independent/self-sufficient/in control, not dependent on, and surrendering to, God's love. Throw in our bent to sin and trying to cover it by the fig leaf of presenting ourselves as a good person.** Mix in some self-deceit and self-pity, being driven at work, some addiction to success even in ministry, and we can see how all this can lead to an empty soul.

And, Satan pounces. In the Bible, the devil is named the accuser, the deceiver, the evil one, the tempter, the liar, the angel of the bottomless pit, the father of lies, the prince of darkness, the spirit that works in the children of disobedience, and in 1 Peter, "a roaring lion seeking to devour our souls."

His mission is to separate us from God, ruin our lives and destroy our souls. He wants us to be discouraged and to think incorrectly about God. He works at having us either delight in our sin so much that we become numb toward God, or feel so guilty about our sin that we hide from God. Satan hounds us at our most vulnerable places, feeding our attitude of self-centeredness, festering our wounds and places of pain, and fanning the flames of our bitter unforgiveness. We must recognize that our soul is the battleground of Satan and Jesus.

All the above realities should motivate us into extreme vigilance in our intention to greenhouse our soul to experience more of Jesus. Be encouraged and take heart: "He (meaning Jesus) who is in you is greater than he (Satan) who is in the world" (1 John 4:4). Jesus' last words on earth: "I will be WITH YOU ALL MOMENTS" (Matthew 28:20), as the "Shepherd and Guardian of our souls" (1 Peter 2:25). As we do life with Jesus, we learn to know Satan's wiles, and we simply resist (James 4:7), and he flees. We learn to discern Satan's lies (like, "you're not worthy," or "If Jesus is so wonderful, then why doesn't everyone follow Him?"). We grow in recognizing Jesus' sweet voice and leading (John 10:1-5). It's often more like a whisper, which is another reason to slow down and come to quiet in our lives. We pay more attention to our soul's longing and let it guide us into Jesus, who alone can satisfy.

**Dallas Willard calls this "the Gospel of Sin Management."*

Desiring and Nurturing Humility

Psalm 51:17 | Deuteronomy 8:12-13, 17 | James 4:6

The desert fathers and mothers said humility is the only soil of the soul in which nearness to Jesus can grow. The word humility comes from the Latin word "humus," which means fertile ground. Humility is being open to God's activity and movement in our lives, readily submitting to His will, not our way, and recognizing that ALL is a gift from His hand. One of the biggest blocks to our experiencing more of Jesus is our DNA of self-determination (control), which is fueled by our pride (I at the center). Andrew Murray said, " … don't look at pride as only an uneven temper and at humility as only a decent virtue. The one is death — the other is life. The one is hell — the other is all heaven." Pride, humility's opposite, renders any dependence on Jesus, and any trusting in Jesus, impossible.

Consider Jesus' humility:

- "He humbled Himself, not grasping to equality with God, but taking on the nature of a bondservant." (Philippians 2:8-9)
- "The Son can do nothing of Himself, unless it is something He sees the Father doing" (John 5:19ff).
- "I do nothing on My own initiative, but speak these things only as the Father has taught Me" (John 8:28) [also John 5:30, 6:38, 12:49, 13:12-17, 14:10].
- Jesus said humility was necessary to receive Him (Matthew 5:3, 11:29, 18:34).
- Jesus taught humility in parables (Luke 15:11ff; Luke 18:9-14; Matthew 23:5-12).

Consider John the Baptist:
" … a person can only receive what is given him from above" (John 3:27).

Consider the Apostle Paul:
"It is only by the grace of God, I am what I am" (1 Corinthians 15:10).

Consider what Oswald Chambers said God said to him:
"I want you in my service, but I can do it without you."

So, how can we nurture humility?

1. Continue to marvel at the grace of God, which is only received, never deserved. "You did not choose Me, but I chose you … " (Jesus speaking in John 15:16).
2. God's in control … ALL is gift from Him (Job 38-42; 1 Corinthians 4:7; Numbers 12:3).
3. We are not perfect people (consider Moses, Abraham, David, Peter). Work at listening to God as He reveals your life to you. Work at confession (Day 25).
4. Without God's help we are a short step away from a fall. Francis De Sales: "No nature is so good that it cannot be perverted by evil. No heart is so filled with God that it cannot rationalize and be deceived."
5. Practice thanking people — a lot. A grateful spirit is humility's sister. Choose gratitude. (Day 30)
6. Do at least one unseen act of grace to another per day … no recognition from anyone. Even, let others get the credit.
7. Embrace those events in your life where you have been humiliated. Some say that the only way to humility is humiliation, because our ego so strongly clings to life. Humility can be grown in us, with the Spirit's help, if it is desired and pursued.

Other Scripture: *Psalm 16:5-6; Psalm 116:7; Psalm 138:6; Jeremiah 2:13; Micah 6:8; 1 Timothy 1:15; James 1:17; 1 Peter 5:5*

DAY 12

The Grace of Receiving

John 1:12 I John 20:21-22 I John 13:8

Our culture's programming (think: "It's more blessed to give than to receive," or "God helps those who help themselves."), combined with our natural bent to prove ourselves worthy of God's love, to deserve God's favor, and to achieve closeness with Jesus, make receiving from God problematic. We identify with Peter when he says, "Jesus, never shall you wash my feet!" (John 13:5-9). Jesus responds not only to Peter, but to all of us today, "Unless you let Me wash you, you have no part with Me." Phillip Yancey writes: "The Buddhist eightfold path, the Hindu doctrine of Karma, the Jewish code of Law and Islam's five tenants — each of these offers a way to earn approval," to achieve good standing with their god equivalent. With Jesus, His cleansing and invitation to union with Him (John 17:21), His Holy Spirit, and His abundant life He's so ready to impart, can only BE RECEIVED. Salvation is not an award to be earned. Experiencing more of Jesus is not gained by getting the spiritual disciplines right. We don't achieve righteousness (the Pharisees flaw): rather, righteousness (or Jesus) possesses us when we accept Him. Many pay lip service to receiving, and then practically live as if their personal disciplines and self-denial will perfect them. Spiritual growth slides into what I am doing, rather than on what God is doing. We believe we can pull our spiritual selves up by our bootstraps. This is a futile attitude. It's as ridiculous as a guy who just received his plumber's license looking at Niagara Falls saying, "I think I can fix this." In fact, and we must hear this, to the degree we feel we earn and deserve Jesus' washing, forgiveness, love and life, to that degree we limit and diminish God's grace at work in our lives.

Marvel how Jesus receives. On that first Palm Sunday, the crowd lavishes worship upon Him (Luke 19:37-40). At the dinner at Simon the Leper's home, a woman anoints Jesus with oil, her tears, washing His feet with her hair (Mark 14:3-9). It's all considered scandalous because receiving grace violates our normal human sensibilities.

To be sure, receiving is difficult. To receive is humbling, cutting against our ego. In essence, we are admitting weakness, inadequacy (2 Corinthians 3:5), and our need for help. We relinquish control and park our pride, giving up fixing our own lives. But consider this: what do we have that we did not receive? (John 3:27). Do we bring anything to Jesus for our salvation, except our sin and wounds that need forgiveness and healing?

It's not minimizing our call to holiness and obedience, or our hope to "let our light shine before others in such a way that they may see our good works and glorify our father in heaven" (Matthew 5:16), when we say that receiving is at the core of our inner life. We'll say it again: We cannot experience more of Jesus by our own will and strength. What a relief! We can only open ourselves to receive what God is doing in us. As Jesus explains the anointing woman's motive to Simon the Leper (Luke 7:36-50, esp. vss. 47-48), "She has received much forgiveness, therefore she loves much." All is gift; our continuous receiving feeds, fills, and fuels our souls to live well, love well, and experience more of Jesus.

False Self ... True Self ... Our Identity

John 13:23; 19:26; 20:2; 21:7, 20   I   Luke 3:21-22

Soren Kirkegaard's first words after his conversion were, "Now Lord, with your help, may my true self emerge." Kirkegaard knew that his true self was the unique self whom God had made and intended him to be (with all the talents, gifts, personality and more that God had given him), but instead he had gravitated to a false self that he created. Kirkegaard is not alone in recognizing that he had a false self, because we all do.

Our false self often begins to take shape in our youth. We might experience a traumatic (even unjust) event or significant deficiencies in our family growing up, which have great emotional impact on us. We learn how TO BE, just to survive. Statements like (not out loud, but subconsciously), "I will always ... ," or "Never again ... " help form this way TO BE. To make it through middle school and high school we become what will be accepted by those whom we MUST be accepted by (the power to belong is strong), and an image (an imposter) of me is born. In college, or in our first job, we figure out what type of person it takes to be successful, and we unconsciously become that person. As an adult, the lure to what one writer labels "less wild lovers" (meaning: lovers other than God) become the goals of our life, and we attach ourselves to them. Any or all the above (or more) could be the origin and the formation of our false self.

Experiencing more of Jesus involves breaking free from our false self. Some say that spiritual formation is just a series of humiliations of the false self. Spiritual formation isn't as much a destination as it is this process of growing awareness of our false self-patterns. God, in His grace and timing, must grant us this awareness. We are like the two disciples on the road to Emmaus, blinded somehow from being aware of reality, with Jesus walking right beside them, needing their eyes to be opened to reality. "You have to know self (meaning claim a self ... be aware of self) to be able to die to self." (Ruth Haley Barton) You can only give over to God all the self that you're aware of.

Part of our difficulty in moving away from and being freed from the false self into our authentic true self, is that the false self has worked out pretty well for us (or, has served us pretty well), and we are reluctant to give it up. Most people have found that when the false self is threatened, it will move into protection mode, defending itself at all costs. In addition, Satan feeds the false self with his lies.

Who knows if Jesus, in His being fully human, dealt with a false self? What we do know is that as Jesus' public ministry began at age 30 with His submitting to baptism, God the Father spoke to Him, calling out His true self, His identity* as a beloved Son, in whom He was bursting with pride. It's stunning that the wilderness experience with Satan's attacks immediately followed the Father's affirmation. Satan tried to keep Jesus from His true self by tempting Him to yield to a false self (identity). "Turn these stones into bread" ... you are what you do;

Our identity — who we are in our deepest place from which every thought, word, deed, choice, emotion, prayer and more springs. Our identity can be dominated by our false self or our true self.

"Bow down to me, and I'll give you all the kingdoms you can see" … you are your position, your power, what you control; and "Throw yourself down from the temple and the angels will catch you" … all will speak well of you and, after all, you are what others say about you. We do not microwave recognizing our false self and growing into our true self. It's a journey over time. Yet, this freedom (Galatians 5:1, 13; Luke 4:18; 2 Corinthians 3:17) from the false self's control is one of the great gifts to us as we experience more of Jesus.

 ## The Place of Suffering
Romans 5:1-5 / *Philippians 3:10* / *Psalm 27:13-14*

Craig Barnes writes in his book, *When God Interrupts*, that he has yet to meet the person who is actually living the life they imagined. Suffering, pain, trouble and affliction happen to each one of us. By speaking of our suffering as it contributes to our spiritual formation, in no way am I trying to put a smiley face on our painful experiences. St John of the Cross said it best: "Suffering is never all right. It's a mess. It's painful, crushing, and can lead to despair." We should never compare our suffering to another's, nor minimize our own suffering. My suffering is mine. Your suffering is yours and significant to you. For many, suffering makes it difficult to trust our loving God, who always has our good in His mind and cares deeply for us. They think something like: "How can He allow the suffering and corresponding debilitating pain in our lives, when He could immediately fix it, correct it, or resolve it?" St. Teresa of Avila once said to God, "It's not at all surprising You have so few friends, considering how You treat the friends You have."

But, suffering holds a significant place in our spiritual formation. In C.S. Lewis' classic *Screwtape Letters*, Screwtape (the devil) is giving instruction to Wormwood (his servant on Earth) saying: "Keep the patient's (us) mind on the unexpected (unexplainable) nature of the trough. God's favorites experience longer and deeper troughs because He cares more about what the little bipeds (us) are becoming, than He does their pleasure in that particular moment." If I graphed my life by the times I was experiencing more of Jesus, and then overlaid that graph with another graph of the times of suffering in my life, the lines would match up … the graphs would be nearly the same. Why is that? It's because suffering has its way of stripping away all the scaffolding we normally build our lives upon. We realize we're not in control of everything. We're usually deeply humbled (often humiliated). We are desperate, more aware of our independence moving toward dependence, as we need God. St. John of the Cross writes "that suffering has a way of breaking us of our vain affections and dismantling our pride."

In deep confusion, darkness, despair and dryness, we cry out to God. **Sometimes**, He doesn't answer or is slow to respond. At the very time we need Him the most, we don't sense Him near; we are totally spent; Scripture reading is hard and without meaning, and prayer seems as empty words. We feel abandoned. St. John of the Cross named this **The Dark Night of the Soul**. But, the reality is that Jesus never leaves us. He weeps over our pain (Luke 19:41-42; John 11:35) as He bears our suffering with us (Isaiah 53:4). He understands our suffering because during His time on Earth He experienced ALL (that means everything) of life we experience (Hebrews 4:15-16; 2:17-18). He carries us through and uses the suffering to shape us, enjoying more intimacy with Him.

Many have come to call suffering "a grace in disguise" because we experience more of Jesus in suffering than in any other way. Some exhort us "to embrace our suffering," "to exalt in our tribulation," "to count it all joy when we encounter various trials," because of its benefits in our lives. What we can do, at a minimum, is remind ourselves when we are under suffering that the reality is: Jesus is near; He's got me; something good is going to be shaped in me; I'm going to experience more of Jesus.

Thomas Keating, in *Open Heart, Open Mind*:

The alterations in our relationship with God are not unlike the presence or absence of someone we greatly love. In the Song of Solomon, God is depicted as pursuing the soul as His beloved. The fathers of the church had a fondness for this particular verse: "O that his left hand were under my head and that his right hand embraced me" (Song of Solomon 2:6). According to their interpretation, God embraces us with both arms. With the left He humbles and corrects us; with the right He lifts us up and consoles us with the assurance of being loved by Him. If you want to be fully embraced by the Lord, you have to accept both arms: the one that allows suffering for the sake of purification and the one that brings the joy of union. When you feel physical pain or when psychological struggles are persecuting you, you should think that God is hugging you tightly. Trials are an expression of His Love, not of rejection.

Other Scripture: *2 Corinthians 4:1, 16-18; John 15:1-2, 18-21; John 16:33; Romans 8:18, 28; 2 Timothy 3:12; James 1:2-4*

 DAY 15

Attention to Our Heart
Proverbs 4:23 | Luke 6:43-45

The sheer number of verses in the Bible concerning our hearts grabs our attention. To be sure, our heart, mind, will, and emotions are all interconnected, but the greatest of these is our heart. The heart is often described as the seat of our emotions, but it is so much more than that. It is the source of our dreams, our trust, our thinking, our feeling, and our actions. One author said, "What the heart trusts, the mind justifies, the emotions desire, and the will carries out." It's been said, "The heart has its reasons the mind knows not," when explaining some of our actions that seem dictated beyond our reasoning to them. The Proverbs verse above states that from our heart springs life, therefore, we must guard our hearts with all the diligence we have.

In the Luke passage above, along with Mark 7:20-24, Jesus elevates our hearts' importance in our spiritual formation. The Apostle Paul says, " … believe in your heart that God raised Jesus from the dead, and you shall be saved" (Romans 10:9-10). As Luke describes the encounter of the resurrected Jesus (unrecognized at first) with the two disciples on the road to Emmaus, he says that they were "slow of heart to believe" (Luke 24:25), and later when their eyes were opened to see Jesus, Luke adds that their hearts "were burning" (Luke 24:32). It's been said that "as a man believeth in his heart, so is he." Jesus supports that reality when he says, "Where your treasure is, there will your heart be also" (Matthew 6:21).

A danger in spiritual formation is to get our behavior right, while our hearts aren't "burning in love" with Jesus. We keep our spirituality on the surface; it is far easier than focusing more deeply on our heart. We can slide into some shade of the image that Jesus presented of being "a whitewashed tomb — real pretty on the outside, but dead on the inside" (Matthew 23:27-28); or, we'll hear Jesus' warning with conviction, "You people honor Me with your lips, but your heart is far from Me" (Matthew 15:8). Dallas Willard said that many of us gravitate to a "Gospel of Sin Management," rather than having a love affair with Jesus.

There is a dichotomy in our hearts. Jeremiah describes it like this: "The heart is deceitful above all things" (Jeremiah 17:9). Out of my heart I can speak praise to Jesus and the next hour vomit against someone who is hindering my agenda. I can speak of Jesus in a chapel talk and later that day lash out in anger at a basketball referee or at my own son for a childish action. That's why King David, a man after God's own heart, prayed, "Create in me a clean heart, O God" (Psalm 51:10). We must join in on that prayer. Later in the same Psalm he says, "The sacrifices God desires are a broken spirit, a broken and contrite heart … ." We can see that any spiritual formation calls us to attend to our inner life, where creating a greenhouse for our heart and soul is our primary concern in experiencing more of Jesus.

Other Scripture: *Matthew 5:8; Mark 12:30; John 14:1; Ephesians 3:17; Colossians 1:27; 2 Thessalonians 3:5*

Spiritual Disciplines for Spiritual Formation

We hold dear a quote from Jim Rayburn (our founder) in Young Life: "It's a sin to bore a kid with the Gospel." I would capture the spirit of that quote for experiencing more of Jesus like this: "It's a sin to bore God (or yourself) with your quiet time." Stay fresh … keep it real … mix it up … try new practices and disciplines. The purpose of the following disciplines introduced in days 16-30 is to open you to God, to receive His grace, to give the Holy Spirit His best chance to reveal the realities of life with Jesus to you. You cannot possibly do all these disciplines every day; but try them, and keep whatever works for you. Recognize that we are all unique, with different wiring, different personalities, in different seasons of life with different schedules, different family situations, in different places with Jesus having different needs, hopes and dreams. God knows you and will meet you where you are. Please don't see these disciplines as more burdens to bear, adding more guilt upon you if you don't regularly do them. These are not "oughts" and "shoulds." We are simply responding to Jesus' invitation to experience more of Him. These disciplines are ways of opening to God and are meant to bring joy in communing with our Lover and Lifegiver, Jesus.

 ### DAY 16 "If You Are Truly My Disciples, You Will Abide in My Word"
(Jesus speaking, John 8:31).
Hebrews 4:12 | 1 Peter 2:2 | Psalm 1:2, 19:7-11

Of all the spiritual disciplines we can do, carrying our hopes and prayers that they would help us experience more of Jesus, DAILY time in the Scripture is the ONE that yields real change over time for every follower of Jesus. Our abiding (making our home) in the Word is God's primary tool of revealing Himself, of imparting His life, and of transforming us (our spiritual formation). There will be times when we spend time in God's Word and we feel that nothing has happened … nothing has changed … no grand lesson was learned. However, we can trust God and His Spirit that absolutely something is happening, often deeper than our senses or understanding. It is like water dripping on a rock. The water by nature is soft; the rock by nature is hard. Daily, you don't notice any change. Ah, but over time … .

What is your view of the Bible? Do you think its primary purpose is to gain knowledge about our God, or to use it as a guide book with helpful and practical words about living God's way? OR, do you see the Scriptures as God's softening, impacting, loving, transforming Word that actually penetrates our hearts (2 Timothy 3:16-17; Isaiah 55:11)? Is reading the Bible for you more like reading a textbook (or, you're always preparing a talk, or searching for some insight you can wisely share); OR, are you soaking in the words of a love letter written to you? Of course, we must study God's Word, understanding its context and original meaning, seeking to grasp God's Story and what the application is to our real lives. But, we also MUST accompany our study with a coming to the

Word in listening mode, taking it in and digesting it. We read being open to the Word so that it can have its way with us. One writer said, "We must read the Word for formation, not just for information." Another said, "Let the text master you, rather than you always mastering the text." We pray before reading, "Speak Lord, for I am listening" (The Father's exhortation to us in Luke 9:35.) We read knowing that the Holy Spirit's role within us is to "guide us into all truth," and "to open our eyes," and to "bring to remembrance all that Jesus has spoken." We submit to what we are reading. If we often read the Scripture without being disturbed, being moved to rejoice or respond, sensing confrontation or conviction, then we're probably not letting the Word sink in (Luke 9:44).

One last question to honestly sit with Jesus around: Are you in love with God's Word? Is it precious to you, a real treasure (Day 15)? Would you say it is lifeblood for you? Read Psalm 119, all 176 verses. Grow to see the Word as essential in your spiritual formation … to abide in it daily … to pray for a passion and love for the Scriptures.

Many commit (promise God) never to live a day without spending time with Him in His Word. Some use prompts and reminders, like "I won't look at my phone until I've been with God in His Word." If you're wondering what Scripture to abide in, there is no wrong answer. The New Covenant (New Testament) seems more relevant and applicable for our lives today; however, the Old Covenant (Old Testament) reveals God's story, i.e., His-story — history. We spend a lot of time in the Gospels because that's where Jesus is. Psalms is called Israel's prayer book. Some read through the Bible in a year, which can be done by reading two chapters of the Old Testament, one Psalm/Proverb/Song of Solomon chapter, and one chapter of the NT each day. The next few days offer some ideas on ways to engage the Bible.

 DAY 17 ## A Way of Listening to God With Scripture … *Lectio Divina*

Luke 9:35

Lectio Divina, "a divine reading," has been around for centuries. It is a slow, reflective reading with a longing to be touched, spoken to, even transformed by God's Word. Lectio is taking time in unhurried listening to the Word of God spoken to us right in our present moment. Some call Lectio Divina a devotional reading, but that lessens the value of this spiritual discipline. Lectio can be done alone or in a small group.

You begin with a time of silence in order to settle. Sitting upright in a comfortable chair with both feet on the floor is helpful to listening well. Breathe a prayer, yielding yourself to God; "I am here Lord and listening." There are four movements.

1. ***Lectio*** (Read)—Slowly read out loud (even if alone) two times through a passage of Scripture (if in a group, have two different readers). Listen as if Jesus Himself was speaking to you. Be aware of a word or a phrase that seems to grab your attention. Don't analyze it or evaluate why it stands out to you. Have a period of silence after the reading of the Word. **25**

2. **Meditatio** (Reflect) — Read the passage out loud again (for the third time). In the silence following the reading, you might ask, "What is going on in my life that makes this word or phrase strike me?" Maybe, you visualize yourself in the story. Maybe you are having a visceral reaction, or are aware of a deep need that this word is hitting up against. Just stay there, "chewing the cud," so to speak, on this word or phrase, resting (you're not uptight) and trusting that if God wants to reveal something to you, He will.

3. **Oratio** (Respond) — You are leaning in. Is God inviting me to a challenge, an exhortation, a direction of thought, an awareness, a conviction, an action, a prayer? It might be something that God wants to enter into with you, to simply be with you. Don't hurry to the next movement.

4. **Contemplatio** (Rest) — What is the "take-away"? In total yieldedness, how is God leading you, realizing that you cannot do anything apart from Him and knowing He will go with you and help you? Linger in the silence.

As you leave **Lectio Divina**, thank God for engaging with you. If there was no specific word for you this time, it's OK; there isn't always. We can trust that something deeper than our conscious knowing was taking place in us. The whole **Lectio Divina** discipline can last up to 30 minutes. If you are doing **Lectio Divina** in a group, you can have some sharing after each movement. It is encouraging to see how God engages each person uniquely in His Word.

DAY 18
A Way of Entering Into God's Word With Jesus

Mark 1:40-42

The whole Bible is the inspired Word of God, but in the four Gospels we come face to face with Jesus. As we daily abide in the Word, time in the Gospels is good, to stay near Jesus.

As you read an encounter with Jesus or a teaching of Jesus, there are several ways to enter in. The Greek way of knowing is the way of scientific thinking. That is, you gather information from empirical observation, then reflect rationally upon the evidence. Then, there's the Hebrew way of knowing. It is the way of story. History is a story. Your own life is a story. In each passage with Jesus, you enter in to the story. You use your imagination, your divinely informed (inspired) imagination. As you place yourself in the story, you actually imagine yourself there. You are hearing what the people are hearing, and you react. Is it day or night? Hot or cool? You feel the crowd pressing in to catch a glimpse of Jesus. What are the smells and sounds around you? Hear what the people were asking the person next to them. Ask what they didn't ask. What are people and you feeling? Thinking? Is there someone with whom you identify? Have fun with this. The event should really come alive.

Read again the three-verse event in Mark above about the leper. (We won't dig as deeply as we could, but just enough to get the idea.) We think that we have nothing in common with a leper. But, think what the leper must be feeling in his situation. Life has dealt him an unjust blow, and he can't just hit re-deal or redo; he's headed toward death, feeling hopeless; others don't want anything to do with him; he feels rejected by friends and even family; he's labeled as a sinner (in that day people thought you didn't get disease except as a result of sin in your life); he's trapped and cannot change his situation; he's feeling helpless and his self-worth/self- image is going down by the minute; he's angry at God for what has happened to him, full of despair, lonely; he feels no one understands or cares. Many of us have felt some of the above, so we can identify with the leper on some level.

He bows down when he meets Jesus. Have you ever bowed down before a person? What would that be like? What does it say about the presence of Jesus for him to be moved to bow down? He seems to wonder what God thinks of him, saying, "If you are willing … ." He asks to be made clean, not to be healed … does he think he's dying and doesn't want to die in an unclean state (a skin disease made one unclean before God)? Jesus has compassion on him. Imagine what it would be like for Jesus to have compassion on you. Jesus touches him BEFORE he's healed. No one touched a leper, because it made you unclean too, plus they thought leprosy was extremely contagious, transmitted by contact. How long had it been since the leper had physical touch with another person? What do you think Jesus' touch did to the emotional self of the leper? Who knows how long it had been since he had been touched, as Dr. Luke called him "a mass of leprosy"? Then he is miraculously healed. What might that have felt like, to be completely healed, cleansed? Would you scream in glee, or dance, or be silent, stunned, numb, trying to take it in? What would you say to Jesus?

You get the picture. This discipline is a way of "being with God" in His Word. Always ask, "So what?" What does this mean in how I experience Jesus? What is relevant today for me?

DAY 19 — A Way of Hiding God's Word in Our Heart

Deuteronomy 6:6-9 | Joshua 1:8 | Matthew 4:4, 7, 10

The naming (above) of this spiritual discipline is much more inviting and compelling than calling it "verse memorization." Memorization brings back memories of preparing (or cramming) for tests during our school years, which was no fun. Plus, most of what we memorized to regurgitate on the test is forgotten today. Don't let that youthful experience of memorizing tarnish this discipline. Though hiding, implanting, filling, grounding, and saturating our hearts with a memorized Word of God is definitely a laborious exercise, the benefits are truly glorious.

When we are under stress or overwhelmed with anxiety, maybe even battling the spiral pull toward despair (and depression), having Scripture embedded in our hearts that we can recall will encourage us. We are reminded of a promise of God, which leads us back to hope, or a truth about God, which calls us to

God's present reality. When we are tempted toward a bad choice or to dishonor God (sin), the Word of God lodged in us can emerge and win the day (like the Matthew verses above). When I've wandered, or doubt has crept in, or self-pity is close by, or bitterness is weighing me down, remembering a memorized verse of the Bible brings back the truth of who God is and who I really am. I can see another promise of God I can rely on, or be reminded of a time when God was very real to me.

Remember this reality: The Word of God carries much more weight and penetrates a human heart and mind, more than any of our human words, no matter how wise and well-crafted they are. So, if someone asks for your counsel or advice, and you have hidden God's Word in your heart, you can speak Scripture to them (not calling attention to yourself by quoting book, chapter and verse, but just speaking God's Word). If you're giving a talk of any kind (or just sharing Jesus with another), memorized Scripture can season your speech. Your message then carries more power as it falls into the listener's heart (2 Corinthians 2:1-4).

Finally, the spiritual discipline of hiding God's Word in your heart through memorization (and review) will actually transform your heart. It's mysterious in that it's not exactly explainable, but it's real. Your heart is changed. "Are there particular verses I should be memorizing?" you might ask. Start with verses that are meaningful to you or that are on a topic you are learning about. As you acquire the taste for memorization, you might commit to a passage or even a chapter of your favorite book of the Bible. "Is there a certain method to share for memorizing?" Use whatever method, strategy, or way fits you … written on an index card and taped to your bathroom mirror, or sitting on your window sill in front of the sink while washing dishes, wherever. Make the verse a song (as we remember song lyrics for years). Possibly use what is normally dead time, like riding in the car (no radio or phone), to review what you're memorizing. You will surely be encouraged and blessed for your effort in this spiritual discipline.

 # Our Journey Into Intimacy With God … Prayer

Hebrews 7:25 | 1 John 2:1 | Romans 8:26-27

Our culture has hijacked the concept of intimacy. Basically, they've sexualized it. But, let's hold onto it, as our longing for intimacy with Jesus is valid and true. Certainly, the spiritual discipline of prayer is the journey into that longed for intimacy experience with Jesus.

Everyone prays. President Eisenhower had it right when he said, "There's no such thing as an atheist in a foxhole." Do you know when prayer first appeared in the Bible? In the last verse of chapter 4 of Genesis. Cain had killed Abel. Adam and Eve had another son. Then it says, "At that time men and women began to call on the name of the Lord." Maybe a child was sick, or the crops needed rain, or Adam and Eve wished for more connection with God, or whatever, but we humans began to reach out to God in prayer.

We cry out to Jesus with a degree of pleading like the disciples must have when they said to Jesus, "Lord, teach us to pray" (Luke 11:1-4). We all have the sense that there's more to prayer than we have experienced. We rarely have the sense that we have "prayed enough," or have "prayed correctly." Brother Lawrence (of *Practicing the Presence of God* fame) once wrote: "I always felt like such a failure at prayer. Then, I realized I would always be a failure at prayer. Things have been going quite nicely since then." We never arrive at prayer. Prayer is a gift from God. St. Teresa of Avila said it best, "Don't be discouraged when learning to pray. Although you meditate, try your hardest, and even shed tears, you cannot make this water flow. God alone gives it to whomever He chooses, and often when one is least thinking about it. Wait on the Lord; persist in prayer without thought of return."

Consider the following reflections. Their goal is to inspire and encourage us to continue on in our praying (Luke 18:1-5), and in learning to pray, may they influence our prayers.

1. We often wonder, "Am I doing this correctly?" Be assured, there is no wrong prayer. There are no angel attorneys in heaven who say to Jesus, "Objection," when say a prayer to God. And, God does not respond with, "Withdraw your prayer. Try again and restate your prayer." Our prayers are always heard by God. The image in Psalm 141:1-2 of our prayers coming to God as incense, or the image in Revelation 8:4 of our prayers being carried to God in golden censors, help us share with God our deepest words. Our prayer does have some power and place with God. All that can be said is that **when we pray, things do happen**, although we may not always see or perceive the answers in the way we've prayed or in the timing we've prayed for. We must realize the reality of Isaiah 55:8-9 while trusting His good intention toward us always. The converse has also proven true: **When we don't pray, things don't happen**. Corrie Ten Boom captures this power when she said, "When Christians meet, Satan smiles; when Christians plan, Satan laughs; when Christians pray, Satan trembles."

2. Our tendency is to have a time of prayer; so when we finish our time of prayer, it's done, and we go on with our day. However, the goal is to let our whole life be offered as prayer. We must break down the wall that separates our prayer from our activity. We share our whole life with God (Day 27). Our living is our praying.

3. We are really praying **WITH** God, not to God. We don't have to come up with the prayer or even initiate the prayer; rather, we are joining a prayer that is already being prayed. That's a game-changer for us. The pressure's off. We can even pray without words knowing that Jesus knows what is on our hearts before we speak it (Matthew 6:8). He is advocating and interceding before the Father on our behalf, while the Spirit is also interceding for us and connecting our spirit with His Spirit. We just happily join in the prayer. That's the reality of today's Scriptures above.

4. Jesus invites us to pray, "Abba (Daddy)." That sweet and intimate beginning to our praying, and the following image, resonate with our spirit:

29

A woman came to see a priest asking, "Would you come and pray with my daddy? He's dying of cancer and he wants to die at home." The priest went to the house, and when he walked into the man's room, he saw the man lying on the bed with an empty chair beside the bed. The priest asked the man if someone had been visiting. The man replied, "Oh, the chair. I've never told anyone this, not even my daughter. I hope you don't think I'm weird, but all my life I've never known how to pray. I've read books on prayer, heard talks on prayer, but nothing ever took hold. Then, a friend told me prayer was like a conversation with Jesus. He suggested I put a chair in front of me, imagine Jesus sitting in the chair, and talk to Him. Since that day, I've never had any difficulty praying. I hope you don't think the cheese has slipped off my cracker." The priest assured the man that there was nothing weird about praying to Jesus and imagining Him sitting beside you. The priest anointed the man and left. Two days later the daughter called to say that her father had just passed. The priest asked, "Did he die peacefully?" She replied, "I left him at 2 p.m. this afternoon. He had a smile on his face when I walked out the door. He even told me one of his corny jokes. When I returned at 3:30, he was dead. One curious thing though — his head was resting not on his pillow, but out on an empty chair beside his bed."

So much more could be offered about the spiritual discipline of prayer, from types of prayer (e.g., intercession, petition, adoration, praise, listening) to fasting and prayer, and more. There are more books on prayer in Christian bookstores than on any other topic. But the truth is, we grow in prayer best by praying.

Other Scripture: 1 Thessalonians 5:15; Philippians 4:6-7; Colossians 4:2

Day 21: Centering Prayer
(also called Breath Prayer or Prayer of the Heart)

Centering Prayer has been practiced by Christians ever since the early years of what has been called "desert spirituality."* The source of Centering Prayer is God within us; its purpose is to usher us into the presence of God, simply to commune with Him. This prayer depends on a disposition of listening with a spirit of receptivity to God, who most often speaks to us in a whisper or with a nudge.

Most of our lives, we are the ones writing the story of our lives, driven mostly by anxiety and our need to control our circumstances and outcomes. In Centering Prayer, we let go of all that into God; we consent to the presence of God and yield (therefore trust) ALL into His care. It seems like such a great act of faith to sit down and close our eyes to the visible, to abandon our "to-do" list, and to open our eyes to the invisible reality of God and His love for us. It is like after a long day, we are sinking into a hot bath tub of God and His love and just soaking in it … relaxing … letting the warmth penetrate all our body.

Desert spirituality is the movement of Christians separating themselves from culture in order to give themselves fully to God. It is also referred to as the Monastic Movement (monks and nuns).

To prepare for Centering Prayer, choose a short "personal word," which is a word or a phrase that best captures your current season of life and relationship with Jesus. For instance, "Abba, I belong to you," or "Abba, guard my heart and direct my steps," or The Jesus Prayer: "Lord Jesus Christ, have mercy on me." You'll repeat, silently and out loud, this personal word over and over in rhythm with your breathing. You breathe in with "Abba" and you exhale with "I belong to you." Your mind is cleared of anxiety and passing thoughts in order to abandon yourself into Jesus. When you become aware that your mind has wandered — which it absolutely will! — you gently release that thought to God, repeat your personal word, and come back to just communing with Him.

Henri Nouwen wrote about why we use the spiritual discipline of Centering Prayer:

"Why should I spend time in prayer when I do nothing in that time but think about people I am angry with, people who are angry with me, books I should read, books I should write, and thousands of other silly things that happen to grab my mind for the moment? The answer is: because God is greater than my mind and my heart, and what is really happening in the house of prayer is not measureable in terms of human success and failure. Only in retrospect do I realize that something extremely important was taking place."

SO, exactly how does one practice Centering Prayer? Set aside 10-20 minutes.

1. Sit relaxed and quiet.
2. Rest into God, who dwells in the center of your being.
3. Repeat your personal word(s), gently supporting your soaking in the hot bathwater of God's love for you.
4. Whenever you're aware of a distraction or wandering thought, gently return to Jesus with your personal word.
5. At the end of your time (maybe set an alarm, so not always checking) whisper a short prayer (or The Lord's Prayer). Thank God for His presence with you.
6. As you re-enter life's busyness, you hopefully will find that your quiet center in Jesus still holds.

A Prayer Walk

Genesis 17:1 | Genesis 5:22, 24
Revelation 4:11 | Micah 6:8

Just a closer walk with Thee
Grant it, Jesus, is my plea.
Daily walking close to Thee,
Let it be, Dear Lord, Let it be
— Old Gospel Hymn

The Hebrew idiom "to walk with someone" (Genesis 17:1) meant to befriend that person on a deep level. "Walking with God" is a metaphor for a life characterized by having an intimate relationship with God (Jesus). For instance, in Genesis 5, the lives of the descendants of Adam are summarized, but it is said only of Enoch that he "walked with God."

A prayer walk is taking a slow walk with Jesus, with the intent of opening your heart to Him in your life's "walk with Jesus" (using "walk" with a double meaning: a literal walk with your dear Friend [in your life-walk with] Jesus). This spiritual discipline awakens your awareness (or alerts you) to God's presence with you. As you begin walking at an absolutely unhurried pace (leave your time piece behind), you invite Jesus to walk with you (Luke 24:13-25). You ask Him to open to you whatever He might want you to experience. You begin to sense your body relaxing, your breathing slowing, any tension exiting, any anxiety fading, and your spirit awakening, but at rest.

You look at things with Jesus and find yourself walking quietly, or speaking conversationally and with blunt honesty, because you know He accepts you just as you are, and is delighted you've chosen to walk with Him, similar to the Garden of Eden walks in the "cool of the afternoon" (Genesis 3:8). You're enjoying keeping company with Jesus, your companion, Savior and Lord.

As you walk, you get in touch with what's going on inside you (emotions, thoughts), and name them the best you can — not trying to fix, solve, or answer them, but just sharing them with Jesus. You also notice everything around you; and you linger, considering the smaller things of nature — the sounds, a leaf, a bug, the sunlight, the breeze and how it makes the grass and the leaves move. Worship of Jesus arises. You realize how all is under the care of the One "who upholds the universe by the power of His Word." The word "worship" comes from the Anglo-Saxon **weorth-scipe**, which means to attribute worth to something or someone. You might read Revelation 4:11 before you walk. Jesus made everything "for His pleasure." As we gaze upon the beauty of His creation and the wonder of His incredible cesign, we are reminded of God's greatness, and that we are a part of His design as Image-bearers. We realize ALL is gift.

As you finish your walk, thank God for His life-giving and love-affirming presence. Carry experiencing Him with you the rest of the day.

DAY 23 Developing Spiritual Friends ... Community

James 5:16 | Hebrews 10:24-25 | Matthew 26:36-45
1 Thessalonians 5:11

None of us can be a Lone Ranger Christian. The sooner we come to the realization that we need others to help us live and experience more of Jesus, the better off we'll be. We call this spiritual discipline, "Intentionally Developing Community" or "Being Intentional in Pursuing Fellowship."

We need the lifting up that only another can bring us when we are discouraged. We need friends in the Lord to pray with us and for us. We need focus when we stray. We need the wisdom and the boldness of a spiritual friend to speak into our lives, especially where we have a blindspot, or have used our keen ability to rationalize ourselves into self-deception. We need "withness" in crisis (like Jesus did in the Matthew Scripture above). We need empathy in sorrow. We need perspective in disappointment. We need encouragement when the weight of the world is on our shoulders. We need to give ourselves away to others in these same ways to "find life" (as Jesus says in Matthew 10:39). We need truth spoken to us when our vision has become distorted. We need gentle reminders and demonstrations of God's love for us when we've forgotten. We need a push when we are stuck. We need to be corralled when we are out of control. We need exhortation toward Jesus when we are focused on self and when relying on our own discernment and strength. We need corporate worship to lift our spirit into His Spirit. We need confrontation when we are out of line. We need someone just to sit with us when we are hurting. We need to be known and to know, at the deepest level. We need someone we can call to share a great joy, who will truly celebrate with us. We need help with discernment in impending decisions, or with how to respond to a situation we find ourselves in. If community deepens, we need accountability in certain life situations. I could go on, but hopefully we have experienced our **NEED** for community, and therefore know that we need others in spiritual (Jesus) friendship if we are to experience more of Jesus.

Even God, in His very nature, has "fellowship" between Father, Son, and the Holy Spirit. Therefore, it's no surprise that we, being created in His Image, by nature, need fellowship.

There are all kinds of fellowship in Jesus and around our common relationship with Jesus. There's the one-on-one meeting where, as safety and trust grows, you can share life and seek counsel; you can ask each other, "How is it with your heart and Jesus today?" and you can answer honestly, without measuring words. There's the small group where Scripture is discussed and life is shared, more transparently over time. A mentor or spiritual director can help you be attentive to God's grace and activity in your life, can help you be aware of your false self rearing its head, can help you discern God's voice from Satan's lies, and can bring you before Jesus in decision, transition, grief or fear. Groups, like Alcoholics Anonymous, provide places where people of like experiences can totally be themselves (totally transparent and vulnerable); and, in their deep, real community help each other through a difficult season in life.

Spiritual friends (community) don't (doesn't) just happen; they must be pursued and cultivated. Remember, like a fine wine, good community must "age." Friends in Christ take time to develop and mature and deepen. Don't get discouraged; keep trying to build community. This spiritual discipline (like all spiritual disciplines) yields joy.

The Furnace of Transformation …
Solitude and Silence*

Psalm 62:5-8 | Psalm 131:2 | Hosea 2:14

If we really believe that Jesus is alive today, that His great joy is communing with us, and that He's always inviting us into MORE of Him, then we must create space to be attentive to Him, to be restored and filled by Him, and to be intentionally available to His healing, teaching, guiding presence. This "creating space" in our lives to give God our undivided attention is called Solitude.

"Time with God" has been vital to us image-bearers since the Garden of Eden (Genesis 2:2-3, 3:8) and the Ten Commandments (Deuteronomy 5:12-15). God instituted rest time with Him, not so much as a reward for our labor, but so that from our rest time with Him our labor would flow. Jesus Himself created space to be alone with His Abba. Stop now and read Matthew 14:23; Mark 1:33-35, 6:29-32; Luke 5:15-16; and John 6:15. Certainly, the never-ending needs of people and ministry eroded His intimacy with the Father, and maybe in His humanness, challenged His dependence on the Father. He needed to be reminded of who He was and encouragement to stay true to His calling. Sometimes, He needed to seek the Father with a decision. If Jesus, who is "Very God of Very God, of One Essence with the Father" (Nicene Creed), needed Solitude time, well then … .

Solitude takes the teeth out of our busyness, which keeps us constantly churned up. We stop the hurry, bring quiet to the noise, and still the chaos of our lives. Solitude is like setting a pitcher of water on the counter top. The water sloshes around for a while, but soon comes to stillness. Solitude at its best is just being with Jesus, enjoying the One who has chosen to live in us; the One who calls us His beloved. In Solitude, the scaffolding that we've built to hold up our false self falls away. It's freeing. We can be real in Solitude, knowing we are deeply loved and accepted for who we are. We are giving God access to the real us, and God is giving Himself completely to us. Solitude is indispensable for deepening our awareness of our belovedness, and for developing our responsiveness to God's activity in our lives. Vance Havner rightfully says, "If you don't come apart for a while, you'll come apart after a while."

Practicing Solitude and Silence:

> In Solitude, we disconnect (we're fasting) from activity, technology, people and words … and, from our compulsion to be "connected."

> In Solitude, we "let go" of everything. The last thing we let go of is our thoughts. Be gentle with yourself as you are distracted with rambling thoughts. If some strain of thought persists, then write it down. Knowing you won't lose that thought now permits you to let it go. Remember that Jesus is delighted you are choosing this time to be with Him. He feels the same way I did when Davis (our youngest) would climb in my lap and be yelling at the other boys, or watching TV, etc. His attention strayed

The title of Day 24 — The Furnace of Transformation — is Henri Nouwen's description of Solitude.

from me, but did I care? My boy had chosen to sit in my lap, and I was thrilled.

> In Solitude, we "let go" of expectations and do no evaluation. Even if we think nothing is happening, be assured, something is happening.

> Don't be afraid of this time alone with God, or fear that we won't have enough to do to fill the time. Begin Solitude with the prayer: "Jesus, help it be enough just to be with you today." This time isn't measured by being productive. Go slow … eat slow … walk slow … read slow. Lift everything into the Father's care (let no prayer go unprayed), listening and paying attention all the while. Pray: "What are you up to in my life?" or, "I'd sure like to hear from You on ____." It's not the time to fix or solve; rather, just sit with it with Jesus. Journaling is good, as is reading past journal entries. Abide in the Scripture, especially the Psalms (Israel's prayer book); abide in Jesus (John 15:4); and abide in Jesus' love for you (John 15:9). Take a prayer walk (Day 22).

Nothing fills us like God's love (Ephesians 3:16-17); nothing transforms us like the presence of God (2 Corinthians 3:18); and nothing replenishes us at the soul level like Solitude and Silence.

Other Scripture: *Psalm 23:2; Psalm 46:10; Psalm 84:2; Psalm 130:5-6; Isaiah 30:15*

 DAY 25

Acknowledging Our Sin Before God … Confession

Psalm 32:1-5 | Psalm 139:23-24 | 1 John 1:8-10

The spiritual discipline called confession is the most difficult of all spiritual disciplines, and the least fun; yet, it is absolutely vital to our experiencing more of Jesus.

What's at stake?

- The fulfillment of all our prayers and longings of intimacy with Jesus.
- Our hope to grow into our true selves.
- The free flow of the living water from the heart of Jesus into our hearts.*
- The reality of living free and not as slaves to our patterns of sin.
- The very wellness and health of our souls.

What gives us the courage to engage in confession?

- Hearing Jesus say to us as He said to the woman caught in the very act of adultery, "Where are your accusers? Does no one condemn you? Neither do I."

---

* *Jonathon Edwards said that having unconfessed sin in our lives is like "standing on the hose" (some water can still get through, but it's just a trickle).*

- Knowing in the "great cloud of witnesses" (Hebrews 12:1), there are Abraham, Moses, David, Peter, and Paul, all who had big failures in their lives.

- Seeing who was closest to Jesus in His day: thieves, prostitutes, the mafia of tax collectors, those who knew their own poverty, brokenness and ongoing need of God's mercy.

- Knowing that acknowledging our wrongdoing and dishonoring of God does not poison our relationship with God; rather, not acknowledging our sin does.

- Knowing God's love for us is not based on how well we live, nor is it diminished by how badly we've lived (Jeremiah 31:3).

- Knowing that Jesus death on the cross enabled complete forgiveness of our confessed sin and its removal from us.

- Knowing that Jesus already knows our sin anyway.

To be sure, when we accept Jesus' gift of salvation, surrender to Him as Lord, and receive Him into our hearts, we are new creatures (2 Corinthians 5:17), beloved sons and daughters of Jesus with His alive Spirit within us. But, as long as we are human beings living on planet Earth, we will have a propensity toward sin. Bernard of Clairvaux captured this reality: "Whatever progress you make while you are still in the body, you are mistaken if you think your faults (sins) are dead" (Romans 7:14-25).

So, the difficulty with confession is that facing our "falling short" is painful. We're so good at casting ourselves as basically nice persons, with only a few hang-ups and minor immaturities, that we've come to believe it about ourselves. Therefore, we minimize, rationalize, cover, mask, and spin our rebellion, bad choices, selfish desires and attachment to pleasure, popularity, possessions and position as normal inconsistencies, rather than the sin it is. After all, we know better. We're somewhat shocked about our sin (but God's not). Admitting our sin to God casts us in a bad light before Him. It can lead us to self-condemnation and shaming ourselves, damaging our self-esteem. True confession is "not fun." However, NOT naming our sin constricts our experiencing more of Jesus and keeps us captive to always propping up and fortifying the image of our righteous self, which is exhausting.

Being aware of our sin can make us "feel" further from Jesus, not closer. But, it's like the light being turned up brighter in a room, which reveals faded paint, a water spot, and a crack in the plaster, all that were unnoticed in the previous low light. Now, they can be removed and the room can be beautified. Where sin abounds, grace abounds all the more (Romans 5:20).

When it comes to facing our sin, our bent ever since the Garden of Eden is to hide from God (God still asks us today, "Where are you?" The parts of us most broken, we keep most hidden.), cover ourselves (fig leaf), and blame or make excuses (Adam: "She gave it to me."). Confession and repentance (the Greek word for repentance is **metanoia**, meaning turning 180 degrees from sin toward Jesus) takes conviction, courage and diligence. Confession is the spiritual discipline, in cooperation with the Holy Spirit, of bringing into our consciousness (John 16:8-11) and naming our sin specifically, out loud. We pray that God would open our eyes and mind to see our sin … to give us Nathan to David moments (1 Samuel 12:7). It might be a clearly seen act, thought or emotion. It might be what's called a stronghold (the Greek word for stronghold is **ochuroma**, which means "holding tightly, safely"), like a lie believed as truth for you, an inner pain unresolved, bitterness or anger, jealousy, etc. It might be a time you didn't act or speak. We could read the 10 Commandments (Exodus 20, Deuteronomy 5) or The Sermon on the Mount (Matthew 5-7) to give the Holy Spirit an opportunity to open our eyes to some sin.

Once you name a sin before God, several things are set in motion:

1. We are forgiven; God does not count it against us.
2. The sin is disarmed, meaning it no longer has the same power in our life.
3. God can begin His healing process, in His power and time.
4. There may be an action God asks us to take in response to our named sin.
5. Possibly, we should share it with our close spiritual friend, as in James 5:16.

How often should we practice this spiritual discipline? Of course, every day we are open to God's reveal (Day 28), but taking an extended period of time for a deeper look at our lives and listen for God, maybe once a week (but, you will find your right rhythm). Confession and repentance is a school from which we never graduate, and rather than a degree we earn, we'll experience cleansing, freedom and an unblocked union with Jesus and His love (Romans 8:38-39).

DAY 26 Granting Forgiveness to Another (or to Oneself)

Matthew 6:14-15 | Matthew 18:21-22, 35 | Luke 23:34

None of us get through life without being deeply hurt. We are simply wronged in some way … a betrayal of trust, an injustice committed against us, a confidence violated, a love rejected or unreturned, an emotional stabbing of our heart, a friend turned against us for their own gain, or a lie spread ruining your reputation, or, being fired unfairly from a job. Of course, more could be added to this list.

Let's say that you've confronted the offender, and they own it and truly apologize. That helps us toward forgiveness. But, let's say they don't own it but turn it back on you, and you leave the encounter discounted, more hurt and angry than before. The offense and hurt drops anchor in the harbor of our hearts. Nothing impacts our experiencing more of Jesus negatively than that deep hurt lodged in our heart. It becomes like a dark spot on an avocado. If it isn't cut out, it soon takes over the whole avocado. It becomes a mess, uneatable. Amazingly, the one who wronged us is not affected; we are affected. When we slow down, like trying to fall asleep, we are either replaying the wrong done to us, rehearsing what we might want to say to them when we again see them, or visualizing their demise. Bitterness is winning in our hearts. Possibly, the worst of it is that the same heart that longs for more of Jesus subtly speaks ill of the person to another and secretly hopes something equally as bad will happen to them. The offender is still affecting us.

We must forgive the person, for our good, and for our restoration and freedom.

The Scripture is clear. Jesus exhorts us to forgive based on the reality that we have been forgiven, and for much worse (Matthew 6 above; Ephesians 4:32). Jesus models granting forgiveness as He endured more injustice, betrayal, rejection and hurt wrongly inflicted upon Him than any of us will ever experience. He prays from the cross, "Father, forgive them, for they know not what they do" (Luke 23:34). And, Jesus teaches us that we should grant forgiveness, no matter what the wrong is or how many times we are wronged (Matthew 18:21-22). Adding further motive for us to forgive, He says that if we don't forgive, then the Father's forgiveness of us is in jeopardy (Mark 11:25-26).*

Knowing Jesus understands our hurt (Hebrews 4:15-16) and carries our pain with us (Isaiah 53:4), is a grand reality to which we cling during this time. Our "granting forgiveness" season of our life can be the most intimate time we will ever have with Jesus.

Intellectually, our mind agrees we must forgive. Emotionally, our hearts are ready and want to forgive, and our wills intend to forgive. But, no matter how hard we try, we cannot forgive on our own strength. Rather, it must be a work of the Holy Spirit in our hearts, and it takes time — a lot of time. We beg God for His help to release the hurt we've been harboring and truly forgive the person. Perhaps, the most tangible thing we can do in the spiritual discipline of granting forgiveness is to pray for the well-being of the offender, for God's favor to rest upon the wrong doer, for blessings to fill the life of the pain inflictor. We pray for these things daily, ONLY IN OBEDIENCE. We don't mean the words at first. But, over time, the Holy Spirit will change our heart. It could even take a year or more, but we will eventually mean the words we pray, by God's working in our hearts.

What if we realize by the Spirit's help that we are the one who caused another person great pain, or what if we get in touch with causing God great pain (Genesis 6:6)? Guilt and shame over our action can be like a ball and chain around our heart. Receiving God's forgiveness, won by Jesus on the cross, is hard enough. Forgiving ourselves is often the more difficult part. Again, this is a work of the Holy Spirit. We receive from the depth of God's love, FOR US.

Keeping Our Memory Alive
Joshua 4:1-8 | Luke 21:14-20

I once had a car accident before the time of seat belts where my date hit the front windshield so hard that it spider-webbed the glass and knocked her partially unconscious. I was not speeding, nor following too closely; however,

---

* The Apostle Paul also exhorts us to forgive in Colossians 3:13.

I was not paying attention to my driving as much as I was enjoying the conversation and activity in my car. Whenever I drove in the following months, I remembered my wreck vividly; and therefore, I was the most attentive and defensive driver you have ever seen. I had both hands on the steering wheel; "Don't talk to me; I'm driving"; I made sure I was five miles under the speed limit with a good cushion of space between me and the car I was following. Slowly over time, I fell back into my less attentive ways as the memory of the accident faded; however, while the memory was alive, my thoughts, motives and actions were greatly impacted by the accident.

We have spiritual Alzheimer's, meaning, we are prone to forget those times in our lives when God was very present and real to us. We might think that if we saw the Red Sea part enabling us to pass through to the other side, and then watch all the Egyptian soldiers be killed as the waters moved back into place, we would never again forget God's goodness to us. We would never doubt His good intention toward us; we would trust Him exclusively, forever after. But, that wasn't the case with the Israelites (Psalm 106), nor is it with us.

God knows how essential our memory is in impacting who we are and our actions in the present. Certainly, the memory of the Jordan River's parting, so that the Israelites could enter their new land through the river on dry land, faded over time. But, the stones of memorial (Joshua 4 above) of yesterday's Realness of God kept the memory alive so that it continued to impact their belief and action. God also gave the Israelites feasts and festivals celebrated every year in order to remember His faithfulness and provision. During the Feast of Booths (or Tabernacles), they remembered God bringing them through their 40-year wilderness journey with manna every morning. During the Feast of Weeks, they remembered God giving Moses the Law on Mt. Sinai. And of course, there's the Passover with its Seder meal. During this meal, the youngest child asks, "Why is this night different than any other night?" Then, the father tells the whole story of God's rescue after 400 years of oppression and slavery in Egypt. Even the Sabbath rhythm (which we've dreadfully lost) was partly established to cease from work one day out of seven, in order to worship God and remember His goodness.

How can we practice the spiritual discipline of Keeping Our Memory Alive?

1. By journaling ... simply recording our prayers, decisions, God's revelations, times God met us or came through for us, and then regularly re-reading those entries. This helps us know God's realness and present day involvement in our lives.

2. By regularly taking the Eucharist (the sacrament of communion, or the Lord's Supper) ... In God's wisdom, He did not leave us a piece of wood from His cross. By His design, we are not sure of the location of Golgotha, the exact place of the stable in Bethlehem where He was born, or where the tomb of His burial is. If these were known, they would capture our focus and worship, as relics and sacred places seem to do. So, Jesus gives us a meal to remember His death for the forgiveness of our sin, and to enjoy the intimacy of His friendship (meal sharing). It is as if He says, "It is My death that I want you to remember. Let My body broken and My blood shed for you impact your life every day."

Eucharisteo is the Greek word for thanksgiving. "**Eu**" means good and "**Charis**" means grace or joy. Deep chara joy is found at the table of eucharisteo, the table of thanksgiving. Many Protestant communities (churches) only offer Eucharist once a month; so, if you miss that Sunday, you go two months or more between memory refreshers. Our human condition requires more frequent remembering. Many Anglican churches offer midweek liturgies with Eucharist that we can attend (even if we are not a member); or, maybe by creating sacred space at Bibles studies and the like, we can remember Jesus' death for us with participating in Eucharist together. Not only does taking in the bread (Jesus' body) and drinking the cup (Jesus' blood) change us; but carrying that current, vivid recall of Jesus' love for us, influences us living the next day, more than we know even consciously.

Other Scripture: Deuteronomy 5:14-15; 1 Chronicles 16:11-12; Psalm 63:6; Psalm 77:11-15; Psalm 78, esp. vss. 7, 11, 42-43, 81; Psalm 105:1-5; Psalm 106; Isaiah 46:8

DAY 28 Practicing the Presence of God ... The Daily Examen

Psalm 139:1-4, 23-24 | Psalm 73:23, 28 | Matthew 28:20

From Genesis to Revelation, a basic theme of the Bible is that our God is **WITH** us. One of the names given to God was by Hagar as she declares, "Thou art El Roi; Thou dost **SEE** me" (Genesis 16:13). Abimelech tells Abraham that Abraham's God is different than any other God in that, "Your God is **WITH** you in all you do" (Genesis 21:22). God encourages Jacob (Genesis 28:15), Joseph (Genesis 39), Moses at the burning bush (Exodus 3:12), all with the reality of His "**WITH-NESS**." Moses' last counsel (Deuteronomy 31:6) to, and God's commissioning of Joshua (Joshua 1:9), is based on the promise that God will be **WITH** him. King David (Psalm 23:4) and the prophets (e.g., Isaiah 41:10) all repeat the same truth. All the way through to Revelation, John says God calls heaven, "Where I am" (Revelation 21:3). Bette Midler's song of the year in 1993 was all wrong, God is not "watching us from a distance"; rather Jesus' last words are our reality, "I am **WITH** you ALL the moments of your everyday life" (Matthew 28:20). In the tyranny of all our urgent, God is present with us, whether we feel Him or not. He's like objects in our side mirror — "closer than they appear." Surely, it strengthens our souls immeasurably knowing that God is **WITH** us in all our moments, meaning not only when we are worshipping Him or doing something for Him, but in the many, many mundane, ordinary moments we live; and, especially in our mess, our sin, our false self-patterns, our ignoring or forgetting Him, our lack of trust, our hurts ... **ALL MOMENTS**. There are no exceptions listed and no qualifications given; it's **ALL MOMENTS**. We don't attain the presence of God; we already are in it. What's missing is our awareness of God's presence with us. The goal is to increase that awareness. Brother Lawrence (the French monk from whom the title of this days comes) tried to maintain an ongoing awareness and silent conversation with God no matter what he was doing. After much time practicing his desire, he wrote: "I actually feel closer to God when I'm washing my dishes in the clatter and activity of the kitchen than I do in the chapel." That's our goal.

It's been noted that couples headed for divorce use the language of "I and me" while couples who have been married for more than 20 years most often use the language of "we and us." In our relationship with God, do we think of "we and us" as we move through our day? A good Muslim will get on their knees and face Mecca to pray five times a day. It is good for us to have some "alerts" throughout the day that turn our hearts toward God. Maybe, before a phone call or a meeting or while riding in the car, we could prompt ourselves to welcome God into the conversation. In the morning during our preparation routine, we could commit our day to the Lord.

The spiritual discipline called "The Daily Examen" helps us live a "with-God" life (rather than living a "for-God" life). It helps us to better detect God's movement in our lives, start finding God in all things, and notice where God shows up in our days. In the daily Examen, we become aware of both the difficult and the beautiful of our day. It may take 10 minutes or it can morph into 30 minutes. It can be done sitting quietly in a room alone at the end of the day, or in taking a walk around the block outside. As you begin, invite the Holy Spirit to bring to mind what you need to see, what you need to pay attention to. Let the Holy Spirit lead the time. Let Him bring to remembrance conversations, tasks, events, thoughts, whatever, as you review the day.

You can ask yourself these questions to prompt the Holy Spirit. Feel free to linger on certain questions as God leads; you do not have to review all the questions every day. Once you've done the Examen a few times, you will find your own rhythm and method.

> ➢ Where was God present today? How did He show up? How was He involved? When was my deepest connection with God? When during the day did I miss Him?
> ➢ What is God up to in my life? What do I need to pay attention to?
> ➢ What was most life-giving to me today? What was most life-draining (or stressful)?
> ➢ What prayers emerge?
> ➢ For what am I most grateful to God today? (Day 30)

What you will find is that by doing the Examen, it actually influences you moving through the next day with God. You become more attentive to living with God, which is the goal. Frances Schaeffer: "True spirituality is living moment by moment with Jesus" (or, in awareness of the presence of God).

Other Scripture: Psalm 26:2; Psalm 84:1-5

Giving Our Life Away

Matthew 10:39, 16:25 | Mark 8:35
Luke 9:24; 17:33 | John 12:25

All four Gospels (above) record Jesus saying that "if you want to find Life, then lose your life (give your life away) for My sake." Yes, that means to die to self and entrust your life to Jesus (Days 4 and 5); but the principle applies to another reality. If you give away your life for Jesus/with Jesus, you will experience more of Jesus as well.

The upshot of Henry T. Blackaby and Claude V. King's excellent *Experiencing God* Bible study was: Look for what God is doing and join Him. In serving God for the good of others and in making God known to others, we will experience more of God. While we see Him work, bring things to be, do miracles, watch Him draw hearts to Himself and more, we will be shaped into more joy and trust. Eugene Peterson says it like this: "God's always doing something before we know it. Therefore, the task of experiencing more of Jesus is not to get God to do something I think needs to be done, but to become aware of what God is doing so that I can respond to it and participate and take delight in it."

For sure, we ask Jesus to show us where He'd like us to invest ourselves with Him. In what other ways can we discern where to give our lives away with Jesus? Frederick Buechner gives us an overview answer to that question: "We try to discover that place of our deep gladness converging with the world's deepest needs." We do not have to look far. Our neighbors and circle of friends all have things going on that the love of God shown by and through us in our unselfish caring (even in our simple presence) in their time of need is a great "work of God." Union with Jesus and our love of God always expresses itself in love of neighbor. This was Jesus' mandate during His last night with His disciples: "By this all people will know that you are my disciples, by how you love one another" (John 13:35). In fact, "You love God only as much as you love the most difficult person in your life (even your enemy) to love."

God made us all with unique talents, interests, and personalities. We all have been given (a) spiritual gift(s) (1 Peter 4:10; 1 Corinthians 12:4-11; Romans 12:6-8; Ephesians 4:4-7, 11-12). We all discern an emerging "calling" on our lives, a place where our heart breaks for God's image-bearers to know Him, a place where when we invest ourselves, it comes fairly easily to us (like natural, like it fits us) and we feel joy. Others affirm us in this expression of ourselves, and we see fruit.

There is no "value hierarchy" around investing ourselves with Jesus. Both the upfront teacher and the one who did all the behind-the-scenes preparations for the room will sense our Lord's delight, and hear Him say, "Well done, good and faithful servant!" As we serve Jesus, we appreciate Him more, depend on Him more, see Him involved in our lives more, sense the Holy Spirit at work more, trust Him more, and love Him more; in short, we experience more of Jesus in giving our lives away.

Choosing Gratitude

1 Thessalonians 5:18
Colossians 3:15-17, 4:2 | Luke 17:11-17

Choosing gratitude, being thankful, expressing thanks every day, throughout the day, seems so simple, but its effects are profound and wide-reaching ... on us, on others and on God. The Hebrew term for gratitude is hikarat hatov, which means "recognizing the good." In whatever our day has been, in whatever circumstances have been dealt to us, we don't have to dig too deeply to find a lot of good, for which to be thank-filled. We can start with the fact that our heart is beating and we are breathing. And, God is present, whether we feel Him near or not, whether good things are happening or bad, "God is present" is our reality. For Jesus' death on the cross for you and me, we daily thank God. Having the scales fall from our eyes and the crust break from around our hearts so that we can see and know Jesus, we thank God. Being thankful properly sets the gauge of our attitude, puts aright our heart to see God's involvement, moves our hearts back toward trust if we've strayed, and lifts our spirits, focusing us on the plus side of the ledger in our life, focusing us off self, and onto God's gifts in life.

The sheer volume of Scripture encouraging, exhorting, and even commanding us to choose gratitude is overwhelming, compelling us to practice gratitude as a spiritual discipline. We can develop "recognizing the good" and "being thankful" as a habit, a way of life.

- It is a basic part of prayer ... Colossians 4:2; Philippians 4:6-7; Ephesians 5:4, 20; Revelation 7:12.
- We see Jesus giving thanks ... Matthew 15:36, 26:27.
- There was a thank offering included in the sacrificial worship of the nation of Israel ... Leviticus 7:12.
- Paul calls a "refusal to give thanks to God" an origin of sin itself ... Romans 1:21.
- And, the Psalms, Israel's prayers, are filled with thanksgiving ... Psalm 9:1, 26:7, 95:2, 100:4, 116:17, 118:1, 136:1 ... just to name a few.

Think humanly how we feel when we are thanked, when someone doesn't take for granted something we've done for them. Not only do we think well of the person (for noticing and appreciating), but their gratitude motivates us to want to do it again. It's the same with God. He doesn't want to be taken for granted. In the Luke passage above, there was only one leper of the 10 Jesus healed who turned back to thank Him. Notice Jesus' reaction.

The Daily Examen (Day 28) finishes (on purpose) with us looking at our life in order to call out things for which we are grateful in that day. We can sense anxiety easing and Jesus' peace falling on us. Choose gratitude to experience more of Jesus.

EPILOGUE

The last 15 days introduced 15 spiritual disciplines (of course, there are many more) to open us to God and to experience more of Jesus. You cannot do all 15 of these every day; realistically, there isn't enough time. We are all unique, and in different life situations, and in different seasons of our lives spiritually. So, we try a spiritual discipline, and if it fits, we wear it for a season of life (meaning if it helps dispose us to God, we continue the practice of it).

The way our days unfold, we easily can have a full day of meaningful activity. However, we must consider: "Have we done the most essential and vital things?" We need spiritual goals (some call these a "Rule of Life") to act as a rudder for the boat of our intention to order our lives, enabling us to experience more of Jesus. Many of us have good intentions and unwritten plans, but they can just keep floating in the clouds unless we write them down. Many of us have written personal goals and job goals, but not spiritual goals. We plan vacations and trips with more care than we do our growing in Jesus. We'll pay a financial planner to help us develop a plan going forward with our finances, but we don't have a plan to direct us toward what we want most: our spiritual development, more of Jesus.

We **MUST** then have a spiritual growth plan. Keep it simple. Don't be rigid. We can adjust our plan at any time. Below is a sample of Spiritual Goals or a Rule of Life.

From September 1 to December 31:

> ➤ Attend midweek Eucharist service two Wednesday mornings/month.
> ➤ Practice Centering Prayer for 10 minutes on three mornings a week.
> ➤ Read a Psalm and part of a Gospel every day.
> ➤ Memorize a verse per week that is meaningful to me.
> ➤ Seek out and meet with a spiritual director/mentor once a month.
> ➤ Find and schedule a "spiritual retreat" before May 1.
> ➤ Have a 2/3 day of solitude per month. Take a prayer walk.
> ➤ Take a walk three nights per week for Daily Examen.

Each goal is a way we partner with God for the growth only He can bring about.

The Two Keys Are:

1. Share your spiritual goals with one other person so they can pray for you and regularly ask how you are doing with them.

2. You must look at your spiritual goals at least once a week (preferably more). If you find that you haven't been doing them, grant yourself grace (because Jesus does!), and adjust your schedule to get back on track.

"May the Lord bless you and keep you; the Lord make His face shine upon you and be gracious to you; and the Lord lift up His countenance upon you and give you peace" (Numbers 6:24-26).

May you experience all the blessings of Jesus (Ephesians 1:3),

— **Ty Saltzgiver**